The Mysteries of the Twelfth Astrological House: Fallen Angels

What people are saying about

The Mysteries of the Twelfth Astrological House

The Mysteries of the Twelfth Astrological House by author Carmen Turner-Schott is a wonderful analysis of an intuitive superhighway that resides in each of us. I have never read an astrology book that describes the twelfth house terrain within the framework of a guided tour of this vast inner universe in such a clear way. The insights in this book can be instantly put to practical use to find loving relationships and to make use of creative energy. The words written by this author inspire self-confidence and are a magical guidance to explore the depths of your own intuition and to walk a path that showers you with mental and emotional peace.

Bernie Ashman is the author of seven astrology books. His most recent published book is *Sun Sign Karma: Resolving Past Life Patterns with Astrology*. Bernie serves clients throughout the United States and internationally. His books have been translated into several languages. He has lectured and taught classes for over 40 years. He resides in Durham, North Carolina.

The Mysteries of the Twelfth Astrological House: Fallen Angels

Carmen Turner-Schott, MSW, LISW

BOOKS

Winchester, UK
Washington, USA

JOHN HUNT PUBLISHING

First published by O-Books, 2022
O-Books is an imprint of John Hunt Publishing Ltd., 3 East St., Alresford,
Hampshire SO24 9EE, UK
office@jhpbooks.com
www.johnhuntpublishing.com
www.o-books.com

For distributor details and how to order please visit the 'Ordering' section on our website.

ISBN: 978 1 78099 343 0
978 1 78099 344 7 (ebook)
Library of Congress Control Number: 2021945123

A CIP catalogue record for this book is available from the British Library.

Design: Stuart Davies

UK: Printed and bound by CPI Group (UK) Ltd, Croydon, CR0 4YY
Printed in North America by CPI GPS partners

We operate a distinctive and ethical publishing philosophy in
all areas of our business, from our global network of authors to
production and worldwide distribution.

Contents

Other Titles by this Author

The Mysteries of the Eighth Astrological House
ISBN: 9781450534505

A Practical Look at the Planets through the Houses
ISBN: 978-1468016246

A Deeper Look at the Sun Signs
ISBN: 1419652176

Astrology From a Christian Perspective

Astrology Awareness: A Compilation of Articles.

Dedication

This book is dedicated to twelfth house people who have shared their personal stories with me. Twelfth house people are individuals who have planets placed in the twelfth astrological house or have placements in Pisces with strong Neptune energy. Always remember that the world needs you. Twelfth house people are angels in human form who fell from heaven to earth to serve those who suffer.

I would like to thank artist Ruth Matthews for bringing the twelfth house to life in her amazing image below titled, *Fallen Angel*. Ruth is an amazing artist from the United Kingdom and is a twelfth house person herself. You can contact her at: rmatthews72@hotmail.com

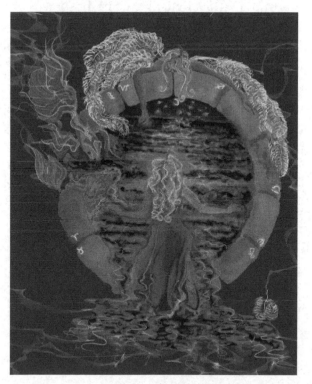

Art designed by Ruth Matthews, United Kingdom

About the Author

Carmen Turner-Schott, MSW, LISW, is a practicing licensed clinical social worker, astrologer, writer and teacher with national and international clientele. She has been working as an astrological counselor and with victims of trauma for over 25 years. She received her undergraduate degree in Psychology from Fontbonne University in St. Louis, Missouri in 1997. She completed her Master of Social Work degree at Washington University in St. Louis, Missouri in 1999. She is a published author and has written five books, *The Mysteries of the Eighth Astrological House, A Practical Look at the Planets through the Houses, A Deeper Look at the Sun Signs, Astrology From a Christian Perspective* and *Astrology Awareness: A Compilation of Articles.*

Carmen has been researching the eighth and twelfth astrological houses for the past 25 years. An eighth and twelfth house person herself, she has personally experienced the energies and lessons of these two very spiritually transforming houses. She has presented astrology workshops for the Association of Research & Enlightenment (A.R.E.) throughout the years and teaches a variety of spiritual development classes.

You can contact her at https://www.8and12houses.com or at carmentschott@gmail.com.

Introduction: Fallen Angels

Angels have no philosophy but love.
– Terri Guillemets

The twelfth house is the most spiritual house in your astrological chart. It is often shrouded in mystery. Many astrology books that I read in the past could never explain the twelfth house in a way that resonated with me. After many years of research, I realized that only someone with twelfth house planets could actually understand it or explain the energy that surrounds it. From personal experiences with twelfth house energy you are able to help others understand the most secretive, hidden and illusive house in astrology.

Twelfth house people are the kindest, most compassionate and sensitive people on this planet. From a young age, you often feel different from everyone else. You might have felt like you were an alien from a foreign land. You never felt like you belonged here on this earth. I have heard similar shared stories and experiences from people all over the world. Many people with twelfth house planets have told me that at some time in their childhood, they often wondered if they were adopted. You felt so distinct and different from your immediate family, that you would grasp at straws trying to figure out why you were so different. A common personality trait that all twelfth house people share is that you feel like you have something inside you that is foreign and different. You perceive the world in a way that is not like normal people. This uniqueness is something special. It is true that you are not like normal people. You often feel like you are from another world.

Most twelfth house people experience mystical and unexplained experiences from a young age. You see ghosts, dream things that happen and can sense when other people are upset or angry. Many people call these abilities empathic and intuitive abilities. It is like you have spider senses and can pinpoint the emotions that others experience. It is no surprise that many people with problems and unhealed pain are drawn to you. I used to feel like there was a sign on my back that said, "Come to me; I will help you." This trait sounds like a positive trait. In reality it can be very painful. The reason it becomes painful is because you often lack boundaries. Your energy is wide open and you give freely. Your energy is like a bright flame that moths are drawn to. You are like a candle that attracts everyone and everything that needs healing. You are a light that shines brightly in the darkness.

You have to be careful how much energy you give and how much you can withstand. By being selfless, you often feel drained. You not only crave time alone, but it's crucial that you make time for yourself to be alone. Your mental health is associated with being alone and having time with your own thoughts. Being alone is not a bad thing for twelfth house people. You actually need this time to recover, recoup and reemerge into the real world. This is why the twelfth house is often referred to as the house of escapism. The only reason you want to escape from the world is so you can find peace. You also seek a connection with yourself and the universe. You love to be home reading a book, doing art, meditating, journaling, writing or listening to music. You love to sit in silence with your own thoughts, emotions and energy. You are completely fine being in the house alone for days. Sometimes you never leave the house unless you have to. You are content with your own company. Many people don't understand you or your need to withdraw from social situations. You often make excuses as to why you can't go out to eat or attend a social event. You know how you will feel once you are around other people, so you decline. You usually want to leave and return home to your private world. You get drained very easily and your energy is sensitive to other people.

Surrounding yourself around spiritual art and music brings comfort. Owning pets like small dogs or larger animals such as horses can be healing for you. Animals often become a surprise therapy pet for twelfth house people. Giving unconditional love is natural for you and animals can be something that helps you survive the more difficult times in your life.

I remember being young, and for some reason, I was always drawn to angels. I was obsessed with learning about angels and I collected angel figurines. Everyone knew the gift to buy for me on holidays and special occasions—was an angel. I never understood where this fascination came from. I was not raised to be religious. I had a natural fascination with mystical things. Angels were one of those spiritual things that I was drawn to study.

Believing in angels for me was protective and made me feel safe. I felt like angels were watching over me, ensuring that I was safe and supported. When I had to go out into the real world, I would think about my guardian angels being around me. Knowing this helped with my anxiety and fears. I felt invincible, like no one could touch me or hurt me. I was naïve because I believed that angels were there all the time to help me. Sometimes when we pray we don't immediately have answers. I finally learned that sometimes the universe sends people as "angels" to assist us and support us in our time of need. Angels in human form. These people often have twelfth house planets.

Twelfth house people are what I call "fallen angels". It's like you fell to earth, to a foreign land. You wander weak and weary wondering why you are here. You question who you are. You feel disconnected at times from your environment as if you are living in a dream. When you are with groups of people you can disassociate from your physical body. You feel like you are an observer and like the world around you is a movie. I remember this happening to me all of the time and it was so hard to explain this experience to anyone. Sometimes when you walk, you feel like you are walking on air and that your feet are not placed firmly on the ground.

You often feel like no one understands you until you find your spiritual circle and group. That is what you are seeking deep inside your heart; you are seeking other people who are just like you. It might take you awhile, but you will find them. You need a spiritual support system in your life to help achieve the goals you choose to accomplish this lifetime. You are here for a purpose. Sometimes this purpose is forced upon you, and the universe strips away from you the very things that you love and cherish. Through these difficult experiences, you often feel that you have to sacrifice yourself, your feelings and your emotions for the greater good. A greater lesson is that you learn that sometimes you have no choice but to let go.

Twelfth house people are giving and enjoy helping others. You like to feel helpful and to be of service to those in need. That is why many twelfth house people and those with Pisces energy are drawn to the helping professions such as psychology, social work, counseling and spiritual advisors. You like to listen to other people's problems. You have such an empathic nature and strong listening ability that others are drawn to you. You can listen to others and offer a kind word of validation, because you truly feel other people's pain. You put yourself in other people's shoes fully. If someone begins to cry, then tears will swell up inside your eyes and you will cry too. You absorb other people's pain, which makes you a spiritual healer. There is a price to this ability, because sometimes you neglect yourself. You may avoid your own self-care.

When planets are placed in the twelfth house, you are someone who wears your heart on your sleeve. You have a very strong, compassionate nature that is otherworldly, just like the traits of an Angel. You often take on other people's pain, karma and burdens. You are walking around on the earth as empaths absorbing all the dark, painful emotions of humanity that surround you.

When planets are in the twelfth house you often ignore yourself, especially when you love someone or when you care about someone. Self-sacrifice is the natural energy of this placement. It's not that you choose to do it. It comes naturally for you to focus on other people and to care about your friends and family. You forget yourself in the midst of your helping. You're meant to help others, but you need to have a good balance. Your lack of boundaries between yourself and other people can cause you pain and suffering. You can be so selfless that you get taken advantage of by those you trust the most. You can be wounded by selfish people who only take and never appreciate or give back to you. This is why the twelfth house is the house of suffering. Feeling used, tossed out, abandoned and betrayed is often a twelfth house experience. This happens when you see other people with rose-colored glasses. You are so innocent that you believe that other people are like you. That is the greatest lesson to learn. The fact is most people are nothing like you and are incapable of the kind of love and sacrifice that you can give to your fellow man.

Even angels need time away from people to recharge and recuperate. Twelfth house people are truly angels on earth. You are fallen angels who wander here helping everyone that crosses your path. You are always blessing others with your vast amount of kindness and compassion. The world needs you, and you are a shining light in the darkness. You show those who are struggling that there is a glimmer of hope. That glimmer of hope is the fact that you exist in this mundane world. You walk among us.

We need twelfth house people to be strong. It is important that you take time to withdraw from the world. This will help you go back out into the real world and serve those who need you. This is when you will feel that you are meant to be here in this world. You will begin to realize that you are a fallen angel. You are not where you are used to being and you feel it's hard and cold here. You begin to realize that you chose to fall to earth so that you could support others, and be a light for them.

You need to allow your angelic light to shine, even if your wings are damaged. You might have some scars. You need to straighten that bent halo and remember who you are. It is not an easy mission to love like an angel, to give like an angel, but you naturally do it. You are God's healers and messengers on Earth.

Chapter One

Deep Truths About the Twelfth House

The twelfth house is ruled by the sign Pisces. Pisces is a water sign and its energy is spiritual, mystical, artistic, compassionate and kind. The planet Neptune rules the sign Pisces and is the natural ruler of the twelfth house. Neptune is the planet of mysticism, spirituality, illusions, sensitivity, escapism, imagination, drugs and addiction. The twelfth house is associated with energy that is hidden and behind the scenes. This is the house of escapism, spirituality and psychic abilities. Having planets placed in the twelfth house can make it difficult to have boundaries with other people. Secret love affairs are associated with the twelfth house, because it is the house of secrets. Secret enemies and secret blessings are all part of this house. Feeling betrayal at times and also feeling that the Universe blesses you are all twelfth house experiences.

The twelfth is the house of service and helping others who are lost, abandoned or wounded. This is also the house of loneliness and the energy of this house creates a desire to withdraw from the real world. Known as the house that rules imagination and creativity, having planets in the twelfth house blesses you with many artistic abilities. The most important thing to remember is that this is the house of the subconscious mind and cosmic consciousness. Connecting with God and the higher spiritual realms comes naturally to you when planets are in this house. The twelfth house is associated with suffering and loss. These experiences often happen to propel you to search for a spiritual path. When planets are in the twelfth house you are meant to serve others and help those who need healing.

The twelfth house is the house of the mystic. You are always on a journey seeking and trying to find deeper meaning to existence. You always knew you had a higher calling from a young age. You often felt misunderstood and judged for being different. Your strength comes after you are tested and betrayed. When you experience great emotional pain and loss is often when you find out who you truly are. You are reborn many times and shed the old self to make way for a whole new version of you. As you grow older, you become more mature and wiser. Just like the shamans and ancient ancestors who used their spiritual gifts to serve their people and to bring hope to others, you are born into this lineage.

As a mystic your path is not an easy one. You will have highs and lows, peaks and valleys, throughout your journey. You will experience what it means to truly sacrifice. You will also learn what true heartache and betrayal feels like. You will also experience what true love feels like and true soul connections. Experiencing deep human emotions will forever change you. You walk forward slowly, step by step, ready to serve and help others who might cross your path and who share a similar pain. Your gift is spiritual understanding and compassion. You always strive to become a better person and you try to make the lives of those around you better.

The twelfth house is often associated with suffering, sacrifice, heartache and loss. The thing you must remember is that it is also the house of cosmic consciousness, oneness with God and psychic gifts. It is the house of guardian angels and mystical experiences. Having planets in the twelfth house blesses you with superpowers and these powers are often hidden deep inside you. Hidden inside your soul waiting to be found are your gifts of compassion, unconditional love and forgiveness. You have been given these gifts so you can enhance them, and utilize them for your true soul mission. It is true that as a twelfth house person you are here on this earth to do special things and to balance out past life karma.

You are here to heal and to accept that some things have to

happen for your greater growth, no matter how painful they are. You have to realize that you are born with a special destiny that many people would not understand or even be capable of mastering. You were chosen to fall to earth and walk among the living in a darker world. Your light shines bright for all to see and many will be drawn to it. You have to let your true self shine, but also need to learn to protect yourself from danger.

It is critical that you learn what it feels like to be hurt by those you trust. This is a special test that many twelfth house people have to experience and pass. If you do not learn the lessons the first time, you often find yourself repeating the same toxic relationship cycles of idealization, betrayal and suffering. It seems like when you truly love someone, they get taken away from you. Sometimes you lose the things that you needed the most. When the universe strips away your greatest treasures, whether they be people, material things or love, you will find that you are left with one thing: yourself.

Chapter Two

Spending Time Alone, Isolation & Solitude

It is critical for me to have time alone all by myself. It is so important to my mental health. I have a special spiritual room in my home where I can go and meditate, read and contemplate my life.
– C.S., Illinois

As a twelfth house Sun and Venus person, I have always felt the urge to withdraw from the world and spend time alone. I enjoyed hanging out with people for a certain amount of time, but even at a young age I remember that I was different. I had a strong need to stay home or be by myself to recover and recoup my energies. I remember feeling very drained and tired after being around friends and family, or after a day at school. I felt better after spending some time alone and in a peaceful environment.

Alone time is healthy for twelfth house people. You need it to heal, recover and survive. You have a heightened sensitivity to the environment. You are like a psychic sponge who absorbs everything going on around you. You pick up on other people's energy very easily. This lack of boundaries between yourself and others was prominent at a young age, even if you did not realize it.

The first time I read about the twelfth house was when I was sixteen. I read about the Sun in the twelfth house and for the first time in my life, I realized why I was different. I accepted myself more and understood my need for alone time. Spending time alone reading, meditating, journaling or listening to music was a healthy way to experience alone time.

The other side of the twelfth house is isolation. The danger of isolation is that you often want to withdraw and hide when you experience challenges in your life, or if you are experiencing high levels of stress. It is healthy to focus on yourself more when you need to balance your life and energies. Although it can become unhealthy if you try to avoid people and places in order to be reclusive. There is a fine line between alone time and avoidance. Avoidance and isolation can be coping mechanisms designed to protect yourself. It can also cause further problems such as loneliness, depression and anxiety.

You need to recognize this tendency in your personality and learn about your own unique phases of what I call "twelfth house withdrawal". Unhealthy withdrawal might include avoiding work or the practical duties you have in this material world. The material world can be a cruel reality and can feel like a harsh place for many twelfth house people. It is important that you face these fears and live in this world.

You chose to be here in physical form. Your soul has to learn to be in the world, but not of the world. Learning to balance your true spiritual self in a practical way is the goal. You are in a physical body for a reason. I remember when I was young and I felt like I did not want to be in this world, because I felt like I was not from here. I disliked practical responsibilities, and it was difficult and painful. It felt easier to join a monastery, temple or become a religious ascetic giving up all my worldly possessions.

I realized that this was not the answer. I often felt guilty for having material things or money. A friend of mine at the time yelled at me and told me that I did not take a vow of poverty. He was right. I realized that running away and avoiding the real world was not the answer. This was running away from my true soul mission, which was helping others in some way.

You are here to help others in this practical world. If you hide away, you can't use your spiritual gifts and abilities to truly uplift others. To walk a spiritual path takes both practical and spiritual balance. When I experienced heartache or betrayal, I wanted to hide. I wanted to avoid people, and spend time with a select few that I knew I could trust. Most of the time I preferred being alone. I stayed home and worked as an astrologer from home for two years. I avoided people and only did consultations online. I isolated myself because I was wounded by people and past experiences. As a twelfth house person, you give a lot of yourself and often do not feel you receive the same kindness in return.

I had worked in a difficult job, with very difficult people, and left feeling drained and hurt. I was worried about being around negative people again. I was very trusting and open-hearted. I experienced betrayal and disloyalty. I isolated and hid for my own protection. After two years, I felt that I had to change.

Like many twelfth house people, I realized that God needed me to go out into the world again. I knew he would eventually force me out. I knew it was because I was a twelfth house person. I knew that my mission was to "serve or suffer". Many astrology books that I had read described this energy and I began to realize it was true. The energy in my life changed and I received my answer. I knew what being a twelfth house person meant and I understood that I had to help others by using my spiritual gifts in the real world. I was avoiding my destiny. Withdrawing became a negative coping mechanism. It became isolation.

I finally reentered the world and began counseling others again. I focused on helping people using astrology as a tool. I realized that being in the practical world was the only way that I could achieve happiness in some way. By being of service, it also helped me heal. This is why twelfth house people attract people with problems from a young age. You naturally attract the wounded because you have experienced wounding yourself. You attract others to you like moths to a flame. Your light shines brightly, and others feel your empathic nature, and kindness.

Twelfth house people need to master balancing time alone and walking firmly in this world. Do not let the negativity sway you from your mission. Your mission is compassionate service to others in the practical world. Having planets in the twelfth house will make you feel like you want to isolate yourself. There will always be a natural tendency to want to withdraw from the world. Sometimes being around people is difficult mainly because you are empathic. You absorb all the emotions and thoughts in your environment. You often lack the boundaries to protect your own energy. Developing a thicker skin is something that took me years to do. Now at mid-life after many years of learning lessons, I try to take better care of myself. Isolation can be both positive and negative. You can learn to isolate to find balance, peace and contentment.

The negative side of isolation is you can become a hermit and never socialize with others. You need social interaction in your life for a healthy mind, body and spirit. You can go days, weeks, months isolated inside your home. This brings you comfort but can also be a detriment to you. When you have to go back out into the world again, it can feel very overwhelming. If you learn to balance the need for isolation with living in the real world, then you will grow stronger as a spiritual healer. There are many people in this world that need your kind spirit, compassionate heart and listening ear. If you isolate yourself and avoid people, then you can't truly be of service.

The need for solitude is something that twelfth house people need to heal and survive. The definition of solitude is very fitting in describing twelfth house personality traits. It is "the quality or state of being alone or remote from society". Another term that is often associated with the twelfth house is seclusion, which is defined as a lonely place. Let's discuss twelfth house people's need for solitude and seclusion.

Having planets placed in the twelfth house especially the Sun or Moon gives a person a strong, overwhelming desire to have peace, serenity and harmony in the environment. Seeking solitude in nature or in your own private world brings twelfth house people comfort. Most people do not like being alone and have to have people around them all the time to feel whole. Twelfth house people are opposite of that. You actually prefer solitude because you enjoy being with yourself. The peace and quiet of your own mind soothes you and is something you like to experience. Maintaining solitude and secluding yourselves away from society and the material world brings you a lot of comfort. Twelfth house people can express themselves in a deep artistic way when they are alone. You will enjoy writing, music, art and spending time in nature.

Many twelfth house people enjoy meditating and finding a peaceful place to spend their time, isolated away from other people. This may seem odd or lonely to most people, but twelfth house people find great spiritual regeneration in seclusion. This is why the twelfth house rules monasteries, temples, churches and places where you can isolate away from normal society. These are places where everyone dresses alike, talks alike, behaves alike and spends time alone in contemplation. Twelfth house people are drawn to these places because it offers them a chance of solitude. I was not raised Catholic, but was interested in becoming a nun when I was in college. I went to a Catholic private college and learned about the Carmelite order and had brochures sent to my dorm room. I almost became a nun. The main reason was my desire for solitude, seclusion and a chance to help others. There was also a sense of security that I felt from thinking of the possibility of being in a monastery. We took a trip to a monastery for a retreat one weekend my junior year and I slept in the rooms where the nuns lived. I read books sat in silence and contemplated life. I journaled the entire weekend and found comfort in that.

Another reason I thought about becoming a nun was because of the strange mystical experiences that I kept having at that time. I was trying to understand my spiritual abilities and I thought that maybe God was calling me to be a nun. This phase ended after about a year when I realized I was not even Catholic. I also knew that I wanted to have children someday. However, that desire was there, a deep desire to seclude myself in a place where I could be alone with my own thoughts.

Many twelfth house people at some time in their lives think about joining these secret societies. You have a need to be behind the scenes. You like to be secluded from the stress, negativity and craziness of the world. The twelfth house is also associated with prisons and the military. In prisons and in the military, everyone dresses alike. I find it interesting that I am a twelfth house Sun and work for the military. I never expected to do that as a social worker, but I actually like it. Any place that is foreign, secluded, secret and invisible is a twelfth house place. Some people with twelfth house planets are drawn to cults or get pulled into them. You are attracted to the spiritual aspect and isolation from the outside world. Twelfth house people need to be careful about illusion, and seeing people as you want to see them and not as they really are. The Neptune energy that rules the twelfth house can cause confusion and pain for twelfth house people. If can cause you a lot of pain if you get involved with unhealthy groups or spiritual organizations.

I met several twelfth house people that were involved in metaphysical groups and it was like they were brainwashed. I have known some individuals that joined cults and had a hard time escaping because of the strong hold the members had on their mind. Twelfth house people lack strong boundaries, so it is important to develop healthy boundaries to protect yourself from these types of situations and people. Some twelfth house people are drawn to occult groups such as the Golden Dawn, Freemasons and Scientology. You are drawn to these groups because of your basic soul need for solitude and seclusion. It does not mean that these groups are right for you, but you may have to learn lessons related to being a part of a spiritual group or religious order.

Twelfth house people are not comfortable being in the limelight. Even if you have a lot of Leo in your chart, and Leos typically like to be center stage and receiving attention. I find that you would rather be behind closed doors. At work, I prefer to work alone with the door closed. I need a quiet atmosphere to focus. Since COVID, I have been able to telework which has made a positive difference in my life. I am at home in my office, no one around, except my puppy Rosie. This enables me to get a lot more accomplished versus being in the office around people and interrupted every day. Telework and the social isolation has actually been a beneficial thing for my mind, body and spirit. I felt like I was able to heal during the lockdown. Prior to the lockdown, I was traveling frequently for work and was never home. The stress was starting to have an impact on my health. I got back in touch with my twelfth house roots last year and I have been thriving in seclusion. I can't even imagine going back to the way it used to be working in an office full of people. My twelfth house Sun enjoys this time of seclusion and isolation. I now have more energy to do the things I love to do.

Many twelfth house people can teach skills to others on how to be content at home, alone, secluded, and how to find peace with solitude. Many people are struggling with being home, socially isolated and secluded from society. Twelfth house people are thriving during this time, because you are in your natural environment. I find that twelfth house people are needed now more than ever. In order to help people around you heal, you can teach skills and coach others on things that they can do when they are alone.

Twelfth house people will always find something to do when you are home by yourselves. You can sleep, watch television, write, take a walk, sit outside and watch people walking by, listen to music and do your hobbies. My husband has been going crazy when he is home. He always says he is bored and I remind him that he doesn't like being on leave more than a few days. I laugh at him and tell him that he needs hobbies. I have a list of things that I want to do when I am home and not working. He is different and feels restless being home, alone, with nothing to do after a few days. It is twelfth house heaven for me to stay home for days at a time. Sometimes I don't leave my house for weeks. I have my groceries delivered to my door. COVID has blessed me with my greatest wish, seclusion and staying behind the scenes. Twelfth house people love to spend time doing all those things you love, alone.

One phenomenon I have noticed with people with planets in the twelfth house, especially the Sun placement, is that you often feel invisible. It is like people forget you are in the room. It is this subtle, awkward energy that happens when you are in large groups of people. The past several months this has happened to me a few times at work. Someone will be talking and mention everyone except me. I always feel like people are leaving me out. I try not to take it personally, but I notice it. When people are supposed to introduce me, they forget and never even mention me. I often feel invisible. I think that many twelfth house people feel this way, and many have shared stories with me that they are often forgotten or not recognized for the work they do.

You can do so much to serve others and achieve accomplishments, but often feel you are stuck behind the scenes. You are out of sight where no one recognizes you or even sees the hard work you are doing. You work in silence, diligently accomplishing tasks and rarely getting credit for your projects. There is something about this behind-the-scenes energy that ends up teaching twelfth house people important lessons. I often think of the quote from Jesus, "to be the first you must first be the least." This motto rings true for many twelfth house people. Twelfth house people learn from experience. Many of your experiences involve being overlooked or ignored. Sometimes I will be at my desk working and people don't even notice me. I can be in a room full of people and it's like I am invisible. This experience is a twelfth house experience. Even if you don't try to be behind-the-scenes and invisible you often are.

There is something about twelfth house energy that transforms your environment and aura. Those who need you will find you and all the other people who don't notice you— well they are not part of your journey. As twelfth house people you have to learn not to take this personally or allow your feelings to be hurt. You have a sensitive nature and it is easier said than done. I know, because I have often felt hurt by this energy. I have felt ignored or not recognized. It seems you are only recognized by those who have pain and need healing. They find you, notice you, and they attach to you.

Chapter Three

Escapism & Healthy Boundaries

I am never in my body and for me it is serve and suffer. I have yet to live my life for me and I have lost everything.
– C.Z., Europe

The twelfth house is associated with escapism. As a twelfth house person you will naturally need to withdraw from the world. When you feel stress and heavy responsibilities you can feel overwhelmed. Escaping from the world is a way to find peace. You are a very compassionate person and wear your heart on your sleeve. You are sensitive to other people's feelings and emotions. You do not like to hurt people. People who are arrogant, rude and unkind disturb you. You like to help people with their problems and you like to be of service. The twelfth house is associated with suffering and this happens when you don't learn to develop strong boundaries to protect yourself from negative energy.

When planets are in the twelfth house you crave peaceful surroundings and avoid conflict. You are very sensitive, and you find it hard to not care. You are kind and sometimes you might feel that other people take your kindness for granted. You are born compassionate and very sensitive to other people's energy, feelings and life circumstances. You don't like to hurt people and you avoid ever being rude, arrogant or unkind. It is very hard for you to tell people that you can't help them. Finding the strength to tell other people, "No," is one of your greatest challenges. You have to learn to protect your own energy, and that means knowing when you need time for self-care and to withdraw from the world. You will need to escape into your own private world so you can heal and recuperate your energy.

The twelfth house is a secret house. It is hidden and illusive. Having planets in the twelfth house creates a desire to avoid stress. When things are difficult you will want to hide and spend time avoiding negativity. You might call in sick to avoid work; you might cancel dinner plans with friends and family. There will be times that you might not be able to explain why, but you will need to escape. Escaping is not always a bad thing. Healthy escapism could involve spiritual pursuits such as meditation, journaling, reading, listening to music, watching movies or just being alone. Those are positive things that you will benefit from doing. On the other hand, when you go through challenges in your life, or if you are around a lot of negative people you can become emotionally, mentally and physically drained. The reason for this is that you are empathic. This means that your energy field is wide open and expansive. You absorb the emotions and energy that surround you.

As a twelfth house person you learned from a young age that you felt different than other people. You absorb everything, and are like a psychic sponge—like a fish flapping in the water with no protection. The lack of boundaries and not knowing how to build protection makes you feel like escaping from people. You take on everything around you and feel what other people are going through. You literally can put yourself in other people's shoes. It is sometimes hard to know what you really feel, versus what you are picking up in your environment. It's important for you to take time to recover your energy. Many people see you as a shy hermit and know that you like to isolate yourself from other people. You only like having to socialize with one or two people at a time. Large groups can be overwhelming for you. You prefer to have one or two friends over at a time. You do not feel comfortable in big groups of people or when too many people are talking at once and things are loud.

When I was in high school, I never understood why I preferred being alone. I can remember being in large groups at school or in a classroom and I felt detached. I did not feel like I was really there. I would start to feel overwhelmed, like I was looking in on myself as an observer. It is a strange experience and very hard to explain in words. The only way I know how to describe it is that I felt like things were not real around me and I was in a dream. I liked to escape from the world in a lot of ways, especially in my imagination. I liked being by myself. I was friendly and played sports and was a part of a team. I liked being by myself though, and I feel emotionally drained after being around people all day. I was a homebody and stayed home on the weekends. I would do solitary activities like shooting baskets by myself at the park or reading astrology books. Escaping and being by myself was something that I always looked forward to.

Another big part of escaping is so you don't have to feel things. The twelfth house is associated with addiction. When you have planets in the twelfth house you will want to detach from your intense emotions and feelings. Twelfth house people like to escape because they feel everything which can cause them to feel overwhelmed. I remember that when someone would cry then I would cry. I would feel everything that everyone was feeling and absorb it into myself. Pisces energy rules the twelfth house, and this enhances your psychic abilities and your need to help others. This is also why planets in the twelfth house create a heightened sensitivity to other people's emotions.

When you have planets in the twelfth house you will want to help people. You want to feel needed. Helping others gives your life purpose. Twelfth house people are here to find a spiritual path. Spending time alone in deep thought and contemplation helps you grow stronger. Escaping through alcohol and drugs is dangerous for twelfth house people. You are already extremely caring and sensitive. The twelfth house is ruled by Neptune, which makes your physical body highly susceptible to any substance. Alcoholism can be associated with escaping life and emotions. It is a way that many people try to cope with psychic abilities because they are trying to numb intense feelings. Alcohol can become a negative coping mechanism when it is used to escape your problems, work, relationships and responsibilities.

I remember when I was in college, and I would stay in my apartment for days. I would not leave unless I had to go to class. If I didn't have class, then I did not leave. I enjoyed staying alone in the comfort of my own peaceful surroundings. I would stay in my pajamas reading books, watching movies and doing astrology charts. I wanted to do whatever I wanted to do and relax. I wanted to escape from the hustle and bustle of the world. I think mainly this was because I have my Sun and Venus in the twelfth house. Being alone was not just something that I enjoyed, but it was something that I had to make time for. It was really a self-care tool that I used to help me feel healthy.

I remember times when my friends would ask me to go out with them and call me to spend time together. I often did not want to go. Sometimes they would convince me to go out to a bar or a party. I would literally be there for five minutes and would be ready to go home. It was not my scene; I disliked being around cigarette smoke, loud noises and large groups of people in a confined area. I remember how unsettling it felt and I had to leave. I would feel drained and exhausted afterwards. The first time I went to a concert, I had my first strange out of body experience. The only way I know how to describe it is that I was there physically, but felt detached from my body like I was an observer to myself. I was looking in on myself and thinking about how everything around me felt fake. I was thinking, "Am I alive? Am I here? Am I really in my body?" It is hard to put into words how this experience felt. It felt like a sense of separateness at the time. Although it also felt like connectedness or oneness with everything around me. I realized that I was not separate at all even though my brain interpreted it that way. I felt that I was broader and wide open connected to everything and everyone.

I always realized that I was very different from other people. I made an effort to use my intuitive abilities to help others. I was instantly drawn to counseling and social work, because it came natural to me. I felt things that other people didn't, saw things that they did not notice. I didn't know why until I started studying astrology. I realized that my Sun and Venus in the twelfth house were probably exactly why I was born the way I am. I would naturally sense if someone was depressed or sad. I would approach them and always ask them how they were doing, or if they were feeling okay. Oftentimes, they would look at me and start crying, and then they would open up to me. So from a young age, I knew that I wanted to be a counselor. I had a lot of people that were drawn to me that wanted help. Many were in pain and had experienced significant loss in their lives. They would tell me all their problems and all their secrets, because of my twelfth house planets. I think they felt my kindness and that I would not judge them. I think other people that need help can sense twelfth house energy and they are drawn to it. Twelfth house people are natural counselors, helpers, servants and good listeners.

I remember my first astrology reading at the age of nineteen from a counseling astrologer in St. Louis. He said, "You have the Sun in the twelfth house and if you don't help people and be of service in some way, then everything will be taken away from you." And I'm like, "What?" Then he said to me, "If you put anything before God it will get taken away from you." It kind of scared me at the time. I had read some books about the twelfth house, but in the 1990s there were not very many good books about the twelfth house. The ones I had read were all about the gloom and doom of these placements. I am sure it scared many twelfth house people when they would read books from the past. Those books would talk about things like bankruptcy, divorce, losing everything materially and death of loved ones. One book even described the Sun in the twelfth house in a way that I will never forget. It described losing everything, and you're sitting down on the curb alone and your husband leaves you, your child dies, you lose your job, and you don't have any money in the bank. You are sitting out on the steps at a park by yourself and you realize none of that matters. Then you feel that you are one with everything and everyone. And you realize that you are a spirit; that you are a soul. You're not a body. You realize that the physical, practical, material world is not all there is. You realize you only have yourself.

This is why twelfth house people have a hard time being in this world and living in it. The world is difficult. The world is painful. The world hurts. I remember I never really was totally in my body. I realized this is escapism in its true form. I was always floating above my body or outside my body mentally. When I would walk, I felt like I was floating on air. I never felt the ground underneath my feet. It was such a strange feeling to experience most of my life. I felt this way until I grew older. I would watch other people stomp on the ground and walk strongly. I would walk light-footed, like I was walking on air. I truly had no control of it.

I always felt like I was floating and I wanted to be above the painful things in the world. I was escaping. I never really realized what it was back then, but I see it clearly now. I was detaching and escaping from having to feel the heaviness of the world around me. As a twelfth house Sun, it was my survival mechanism. It helped me survive in a painful world where I felt everyone's pain. Being outside my body was a way of protecting myself because I didn't have to feel as much. It was my defense mechanism of dealing with my empathic abilities. I always tried to have a barrier around myself. I remember sitting in class and imagining a yellow bubble of light around myself or a mirror where everyone's emotions would reflect off of me. I did this to help myself when I was in groups of people because I would feel uncomfortable and tired.

I remember one time when I was in a mystical bookstore there was a male psychic who everyone was afraid of. He was quiet, tall and did not speak much. Everyone perceived him as intense. One day I was in the store buying a book and he was there. He looked at me and yelled, "You need to be in your body. You are not in your body because you are up above it. You chose to be here. You need to be in your body!" I told him that I didn't want to be in my body because it hurt too much. He told me, "If you don't ground yourself and be in your body then you will not live here very long." That stuck with me. After that conversation, I realized that escaping and detaching was not always a healthy coping mechanism. I started practicing being grounded. I started doing a tree meditation and breathing exercises. This helped me not escape and allowed myself to feel things fully. This helped me become a stronger person. Now that I am older, I feel that I am fully in my body. I overcame that personality trait with practice.

I never escaped through drugs or alcohol. A lot of people that I know with twelfth house planets have struggled with addiction. The twelfth house rules addiction and especially alcoholism, because it is a way to numb the emotions. Some people I knew did experiment. I knew I was already strange and different, so I never had any thoughts to try any drugs. I was very spiritual and had a very creative mind. I already had a very vivid imagination from a young age. I would have vivid visions, flashes and deep dreams. If someone told me something, then I would see it visually in my mind vividly and intensely. I did not need to experiment with drugs or alcohol to escape. I was already able to escape within my imagination and mind.

A lot of clients I have worked with over the past 25 years have shared their struggles with addiction with me. Many of them were twelfth house people. Sometimes you might use drugs to escape from your painful emotions or you might try them to have mystical experiences or heighten your psychic abilities. One of the biggest lessons you need to learn is that you need to develop healthy coping skills and healthy boundaries when you have planets placed in the twelfth house.

When planets are in the twelfth house, you might hide inside your house and never answer the phone until you really want to. You may want to hide and not have to interact with people. To survive in this world you learned quickly that you needed to make money, pay bills, and take care of yourself. Some twelfth house people find this reality hard to accept. It can be difficult for you to live like normal in this world, because you are not normal. You are special and blessed with a special life purpose. When you were younger you were able to hide more because you did not have to struggle to survive on your own. As you get older and become an adult, you can't hide anymore. Some twelfth house people thrive at work. Some can have successful careers while others find it difficult to adhere to society's rules and class system. You may choose not to work but prefer to stay home and write or create art all day. You might pursue your spiritual path and spiritual hobbies full-time. You may decide to work a part-time job to make ends meet. You find contentment pursuing creative outlets. It is not about making money to you because it's about expressing your imagination. Although, if you could make money doing something that you love, then you would happily accept that. Money might be scarce at times, but you prefer to feel peaceful by being spiritual. You love to have the freedom to be who you truly are.

Twelfth house people need to remember that you have to learn to live in this world, but you should not let the world get into you. This can be hard for you to figure out and balance. A lot of twelfth house people are tested, and do better when they release the pressures of the world. Escaping through spiritual pursuits such as meditation, yoga, deep breathing, energy healing and contemplation are all beneficial for twelfth house people. In India, they call this philosophy dharma, which means being in the world, but not of the world. I think the wisdom here is for twelfth house people to remember to stay spiritual, and that they don't have be practical all the time. Being trapped in worldly concerns, and allowing them to stress you out, can kill your spirit. It hurts your soul and hurts you. You have to feel free to be weird, creative and imaginative. You want to be spiritual. You want to talk about astrology. You want to talk about past lives, and research why you are here on this earth. You want to talk about ghosts, crystals, spirits and mediumship. You might even be fascinated with UFOs and extraterrestrials. You may believe you have even seen a UFO yourself. Many twelfth house people have real experiences with these supernatural things, and to you, it is your reality. You love the mystical side of life because it makes you feel alive.

You will have difficulty working a nine-to-five job, and focusing on mundane things day to day. You need more in your life. You feel that you are fulfilling your higher purpose. You cannot live in the practical world full-time. You have to be spiritual and it's your mission as a twelfth house person to serve or suffer. Learning to help others in some way, using your gifts to help others heal, will help bring you blessings. Escaping from the world in healthy ways will help you handle your special gifts.

Chapter Four

True Love: Seeking a Soul Mate Connection

One of the first articles that I wrote was about having Venus in the twelfth house. I wrote about how many times twelfth house people shared with me their struggles with relationships. A common theme involved feelings of heartbreak and feeling abandoned. There are both positive and negative things about planets in the twelfth house. One thing I have found through my research is that you will at some time in your life experience betrayal and heartbreak in personal love. I find that twelfth house people have a difficult time letting go of past love and relationships. They hold on to the positive memories and often ignore or block out the more negative experiences that they have lived through. They are known to make excuses for certain relationship partners. Twelfth house people are always seeking true love and a soul mate. This is something that I did myself when I was younger. I learned this lesson, the hard way. It took many years to truly learn what this placement was trying to teach me. It was not an easy journey, and it was a struggle each step of the way. When looking back now and when I look in the mirror, I see a completely different person looking back at me. I see a person who has scars, wounds, and memories but survived them.

When Venus is in the twelfth house, you will resonate greatly with this chapter. Other planets in the twelfth house can also create similar experiences and energy throughout your life. Honestly, I have seen that Venus in the twelfth house is challenging. I did not see the positive side of having this placement until I got older. I realized that there are also positive blessings with having Venus in the twelfth. Sometimes it takes time to see it.

When you have twelfth house planets, you are influenced greatly by the planet Neptune. You will be prone to illusions when it involves love. You listen to your heart, and when you feel love for someone, there is nothing that will stop you from expressing it. The problem is that you can attract people that are not worthy of your love. You can fall in love with someone who is not free to be with you. Twelfth house people seek a soul mate and twin flame. You may feel that you have lived past lives and you have loved this person in the past. You have a restless soul that seeks connection and oneness with others. You will be on a mission to connect and seek true love.

You can be very idealistic when it comes to love. You often believe that God has a special person in the world that was made just for you. You can spend a lot of time seeking this special person. As a twelfth house person, I remember how I always wanted to find someone to love. I had many crushes growing up. The serious relationships that I had in high school were all committed and long-term. At that time I never really felt true love or a deep connection to anyone. I felt restless and was always seeking that special feeling that I believed was true love. I was never content, but simply going through the motions trying to force something that was not meant to be. Some of the relationship partners that I attracted were not good for me. I experienced a lot of heartache in love due to my idealism. I would idolize people and ignore all the red flags that I would see at the beginning of the relationship. I got my heart broken by people who never truly were capable of loving me with the same depth.

A lot of twelfth house people tell me that they feel that love is the most painful experience that they have had to go through. You may have your heart broken more than once. You may start feeling disillusioned about love in general. As a twelfth house person you will always try to figure out what true love is. You may feel that it is something that you will know and feel inside.

29

You might believe that it involves experiencing passion and sexual chemistry. You might believe love is more of a spiritual connection with natural intimacy. You believe you should feel a special bond. You might feel like you have known each other for lifetimes. As a twelfth house person you will seek this kind of connection with another person. You will believe that you have to feel strong emotions in order to be in love.

Twelfth house people love others very deeply and on a spiritual type of level. You will often feel love and passion with those who are wounded. Many people that you feel love for have deep problems, and need healing. After my own experiences and counseling twelfth house people, I have witnessed these situations with many clients. If you have planets in the twelfth house, you often fall in love with others that don't love themselves, or they are incapable of loving you. You love these people so much, that you can lose yourself in them. You might make them the focus of your life. You put your lover on a pedestal, and seek only to make them happy. As a result, you often suffer and sacrifice your own happiness.

You might believe that you found your soul mate. You feel it's destiny and that God has sent you this special person. You may believe you were meant to be with them. The truth is, that it's not always true love. It is your twelfth house gifts that attract these strong bonds. You can sometimes feel like a victim, or feel betrayed. Betrayal happens in your life when you do not expect someone that you love, and care for, to leave you. You can feel abandoned, and cast out by those you loved the most. Feelings of betrayal are strong for twelfth house people. You give your heart, soul and full trust to those you love. You trust people so much that you never expect them to hurt or mislead you. This is why it's so painful for twelfth house people to be betrayed. Your naïve trust and belief that others always have good intentions can backfire on you, causing lasting pain. Betrayal cuts you deeply, and creates a wound that sometimes is never fully healed.

You are a kind soul who trusts others, but you can be vulnerable to people who are charming and narcissistic. Unhealthy people see your light and unconditional love. They may try to manipulate you and take advantage of your kindness. Sometimes people are attracted to you because they sense that you have something special, and they want to possess it. You are like a beautiful flower in a garden that they really want to pick. Once they get what they want from you or grow bored, they might drop you and disappear. You might feel that one day they love you, and then the next day you mean nothing to them. At least that is the way that some people make twelfth house people feel. When you have planets in the twelfth house, you will most likely experience a one-sided relationship at some time in your life. This is why the twelfth house is often associated with secret love affairs and heartache. Many times there is a lack of reciprocation in love.

When planets are placed in the twelfth house you will need to realize that true love can only be found by loving yourself, valuing yourself and accepting your own biases concerning love. When you love who you are then you will realize the value of creating strong boundaries around yourself. You will learn and believe that you deserve love that is reciprocated. You deserve to be treated as kindly as you treat others. You deserve to experience deep friendship and loyalty with someone you can rely on. It is important to start loving those people who have proved their worth and loyalty. Twelfth house people need to learn to love those around them. They sometimes do not see those who truly love them, who are right in front of them because they are seeking this soul mate love that they believe exists. When you learn to love those who are around you and those who are there for you during traumatic situations or personal struggles, then you will begin to learn what true love is.

Your greatest lesson as a twelfth house person is to learn the truth about romantic love. Your search for a deep soul connection often happens with those who are incapable of loving you in the same way you love them. The reason this happens is that they are not on the same level as you. Most people are not on the same spiritual, emotional or mental level as twelfth house people. Once you realize the truth of why you are attracted to certain people and learn to develop stronger boundaries, then you will learn to believe in yourself. You are a fallen angel in human form capable of great unconditional love. Most normal people are not able to love like you. You truly can be a living example of God's love.

As a twelfth house person, you are loyal to a fault. People can betray you and hurt you deeply, and make you feel like you meant nothing to them. An interesting phenomenon occurs for many twelfth house people. You often find that those who abandoned and hurt you the most seem to always return. They come back into your life years later to apologize, and seek repentance. They will tell you how they never meant to hurt you and express how sorry they are. My advice for twelfth house people is not to forget too easily. You need to try to remember that how people treat you is a large sign. Behavior is difficult to change. You can forgive others, but it does not mean that you have to allow them back into your life. You often learn this lesson the hard way. You allow people who have wounded you back into your life, and you forgive them. It is no surprise that the same thing often happens again. You find yourself discarded and neglected once again. This brings up the same old wounds of heartbreak that they caused you in the past. You want to believe that people change and always seek to see the good in people.

You might wonder why this same type of experience happens to you. The lesson for twelfth house people is to learn to love themselves first. You are meant to realize that you are your own soul mate. You are also meant to love others in a spiritual way that goes beyond the physical. This is why so many people with hidden pain, secrets and wounds are attracted to you. They seek you out, for you to help them heal their problems. Other people sense that you love unconditionally. Your gift to the world is your natural talent of unconditional love.

As a twelfth house person, once you realize what love really is and learn that lesson, then you will break the negative karmic pattern. The painful cycle of relationship suffering will fade away and you will rise above it, and heal. You will transform when you realize that all those people who caused you heartache and pain can be accepted as a learning lesson. These people never deserved you in the first place. They were never on your level. They can never love you the way that you love them. Once twelfth house people realize this truth you will feel great responsibility. It can be lonely when you realize that you are here for a special mission, and accept that you are different than most people. This is why loneliness is often associated with the twelfth house.

You are from a different world and it reminds me of the story of Judas and Jesus. Jesus loved Judas but he betrayed Jesus with a kiss. This historic moment can be seen throughout the world in many different paintings. It always reminded me of the twelfth house. Jesus and Christianity itself are symbolized by the two fish. Similar to the energy of the sign Pisces, the fish that rules the twelfth house. This story symbolizes twelfth house energy and experiences. Many twelfth house people never expect to be hurt or betrayed by someone that they were loyal to and loved. You feel that you would have done anything for the people that have hurt you. You are loyal to a fault. You often feel like you never get the same amount of loyalty returned to you.

The lesson here is that you have to realize that you are born alone. When you die, you will take no one else with you. It is important to remember to love those that are around you.

Cherish your family, friends and those who come to you for guidance day to day in your normal surroundings. Developing a practical view of love will help you transform your belief in the notion of true love, soul mates and all the magical fairy tale love stories.

Chapter Five

Overcoming Heartbreak & Loss

I never realized how hard it would be to move forward. I think the main reason I struggled was because we shared physical intimacy. I bonded with him, and believed he loved me and would change his life for me. In reality, he just used me for sex. My intensions were pure, but his were never pure. That is something that hurt deeper than I can explain once I realized the truth.
– L.M.B., Missouri

The most important way to move forward in your life after heartbreak is by focusing on yourself. I am going to discuss practical tips that might help you overcome the hurt, betrayal and heartache from karmic relationships. As a twelfth house person, you might find that it takes you longer than most people to heal and move forward from the past. Your friends and family might not understand you. They may grow impatient with you in terms of how slowly you move forward from bad experiences. As a twelfth house person myself, I know how hard it is to truly let go of memories even if they are painful. It takes us more time than most people to heal and overcome heartbreak. In the last chapter, we talked about how twelfth house people search for true love and a soul mate. In this chapter, we will focus on specific skills that you can implement in your life to truly understand the past, and move forward towards a brighter future.

The first skill that twelfth house people need to develop is to take the rose-colored glasses off and stop romanticizing other people. I can tell you firsthand as a Sun and Venus in the twelfth house person that I would put people up on a pedestal. I would only focus on the good things about the person, even if their actions proved to me to be opposite of my beliefs. I know the pain of losing love and feeling used by someone you trusted. I know how it feels to love someone who does not love you back, or love someone who abandons and takes you for granted. It is one of the greatest lessons that twelfth house people have to experience.

I know the pain in your heart. I know how it feels and I don't wish that pain on anyone. It is beyond words. It is hard to describe to someone who has not experienced it. Twelfth house people learn the hard way by giving too much of themselves. Your friends might warn you, tell you that your partner is not treating you well but you won't listen. You might have experienced that your family was concerned that someone is not good for you, but you will not see it yourself. You wear rose-colored glasses like a true twelfth house person. This is part of who you are. The term "love is blind" rings true here.

Many twelfth house people tell me they have gone through this experience multiple times, and ended up getting really hurt. I can tell you that I don't know if my advice will help you, but I want to share some things with you that I have learned as a twelfth house person. Learning to heal my wounds related to love took me many years. I realize that some of my wounds from heartbreak are still affecting me, even after all these years. Memories sometimes pop up and haunt me. I even dream about people who have hurt me. You know your heart is pure. Twelfth house people often agree with me that the heart never forgets.

One of the first ways to overcome heartache is something that was told to me and was hard for me to believe myself. I did not agree when a friend would say it to me or if someone was trying to comfort and help me. I would get defensive when they would say it, but now looking back I know it's true. The number one way to heal and move forward is by giving it time. As they say, time heals all wounds. I never liked that saying, but now I believe it's true. The more time that goes by, the more you grieve, and allow yourself to feel the different emotions, then the less they will impact you. The more time goes by, and the more you get up and move forward every day, then the more you slowly forget the hurt. You will try to move forward slowly, taking baby steps. Sometimes you take two steps forward and then three steps back. It is okay and remember not to beat yourself up too much. Time helps this process.

Sometimes the heartbreak that twelfth house people have experienced leaves scars. When you have a wound, such as when you get cut with a knife, then it leaves a scar on your body. The same is true for heartbreak. You may heal that heartbreak on the surface, but you always have a reminder, or memory of it in a scar on your heart. This scar is left behind to remind you of that lesson and learning. The lesson that we talked about is to stop romanticizing other people, and putting them up on a pedestal. Stop loving other people more than you love yourself. You need to start seeing people in a realistic and practical way. People are human and they have flaws, even those people you love so deeply. Another good tip is to always recognize that you can be hurt. The first heartbreak is often the most painful for twelfth house people. The reason it hits you the hardest is because you were living in a fantasy world. You believed that everyone was as honest, pure and compassionate as you were. You learned the truth the hard way, through direct experience.

As a twelfth house person you see the good in everyone. When you heard other people's problems you used to believe that no one would ever do those things to you. Hearing the stories other people shared with you was not even enough to protect you from believing that the world could be a dangerous, and hurtful, place. I used to be so naïve and sheltered. Looking back, I realize I was living in a fantasy world most of my life until I was older. I don't know how I survived so long that way. I had no fear and always had this innocent belief in the good. I believed that angels were protecting me, and that my guardian angels would be with me even if I was in a dangerous situation. I have heard it all, so many terrible stories of pain and abuse at the hands of people that twelfth house people trusted. Nothing shocks me anymore. The thing twelfth house people need to realize is that not everyone has a heart like yours.

You never believed anyone would hurt you. It's one of the blessings of the twelfth house—your kindness and trusting nature. You can be too trusting to the wrong types of people. Many twelfth house people feel they are alone. You often feel like you are drowning in your emotional pain, and no one is truly there for you when you need them. Twelfth house people replay scenarios in your head, reliving and imagining the memories that you had with people who hurt you. You tend to only remember the good things, and remember the romantic feelings that you felt. You often avoid and develop illusions around the truth. You do not want to remember the bad things that happened in relationships. You have to learn to let go. It can take you a lot longer, in my perspective, to heal and let go of past love. Many people will never understand this about you. Once you accept this part of yourself, then you will feel relieved. You are not alone. You have many other twelfth house people who understand. Many twelfth house people feel exactly the same way as you do. You just might not have met them yet.

I have met a lot of twelfth house people in the past 25 years since I started practicing astrology. I have seen a lot of astrology charts, and let me tell you the truth, most people that have a hard time letting go of heartbreak have twelfth house planets, Pisces energy, or heavy Neptune energy. It might be more difficult for you to let go, but you can do it. I know it's possible, because I had to do it several times. Sometimes it took me three years, sometimes five years before I could let go. I look back and realize how much precious time that I wasted by focusing my thoughts and feelings on people that never truly cared about me. It was all about one-sided love relationships. It took me years to admit it to myself. For me it was never a short six-month thing, it always took years to heal. I would wallow in my emotions, by replaying in my head the wonderful memories. I would remember the love that I felt and then the pain I felt losing that person. I hear similar things from twelfth house clients. They ask me, "Do they still love me? Did they ever love me? How could they do this to me?" My advice is always the same and I explain to them that they cared too much. You need to hear these words and believe them, "You care too much about others, and not enough about yourself!" Let that sink in.

I have to laugh, because I know how true it is. My own daughter would tell me that I was too nice or I cared too much. She would warn me that I am too trusting. She would have feelings about certain people in my life and she would be suspicious of people that I called friends. Many times her feelings were accurate. You should not change your compassionate and kind nature. You should not allow the pain that others have caused you to transform you into a negative untrusting person. That is not the destiny of a twelfth house person. You do have to start seeing the world in a more realistic, practical way so you can protect yourself.

Twelfth house people are kind to a fault and born with natural genuine kindness. You always care, and you can't become numb and be a robot. You are never going to be able to cut people off like a Scorpio unless you have a lot of Scorpio energy. Even if you do, if it's in the twelfth house, it might be more difficult for you to do so. It might never be easy for you to be able to just let go of people, and walk away. Twelfth house people typically sacrifice themselves for love. You sacrifice yourself to help and take care of other people. You often give your love and attention to those who are opportunists. These people see you coming a mile away. They know that you will forgive them and that you will do everything for them. As twelfth house people you wear your heart on your sleeve. This can make you an easy target for people who are looking to benefit from or use others for their own gain. I can't believe I am writing this, but I have come to realize it's true. In the past, my twelfth house self would think that this was a mean thing to say.

Twelfth house people often live in an illusion. The second lesson to learn is to stop sacrificing yourself for other people. Start loving yourself and start making sacrifices that benefit you instead of others. You don't have to always put other people first. You are a natural at serving others and helping people. That is your gift but you have to love yourself fully and that means understanding your own needs and wants. You have to work on feeling good about focusing on your own needs, and doing things to fulfill them yourself. As a twelfth house person, for most of my life I never stood up for myself. I allowed other people to walk all over me. I used to say to people, "Please don't take my kindness as a weakness." I knew my own weaknesses and they were that I was too nice and forgave too easily. It sounds crazy to most people, but twelfth house people know exactly what I am talking about.

Now that I am older, I am standing up for myself more. In the past, I felt that I was weak and my feelings were hurt so easily. I would cry at the drop of a hat. If someone else was hurting, I would tear up. I am a lot different now. I have a thicker skin and have toughened up a bit. However, even though I have toughened my skin, I still care too much. Twelfth house people are caring; you can't change that about yourself and you should not want to. Your gift is that you care about others. It is not a bad thing to care, but you just have to know and understand yourself. The key for your survival is to develop strong boundaries. Almost every twelfth house person I know has admitted to me that they struggle with developing boundaries and keeping healthy boundaries with other people.

Twelfth house people have illusions, fantasies and delusions. You believe that people are good at heart and similar to you.

Then reality hits, and you realize that not all people are kind. When you experience these realities you are devastated— absolutely fractured. You just don't understand it. You tend to escape from it. Twelfth house people have escapist tendencies as we discussed earlier. This can be both a positive and negative coping mechanism. Sometimes escapism leads to depression, loneliness and feeling disconnected from others. You may start to isolate yourself too much. You can't avoid your feelings forever. You have to eventually face your jaded feelings and learn how to feel normal again.

I am going to tell you some things that helped me heal from heartbreak. I know what it feels like. I know what it's like to hurt, and suffer in silence because you are hiding from everyone how terrible you feel. You struggle in private, and then put on a brave smile in front of the world. No one would ever know how messed up and emotionally devastated you are. I started my twelfth house Facebook group in 2011 to be able to connect with other people who have been through similar experiences and felt the same way about life in general. I met many people with twelfth house planets from all over the world and they would post and share their struggles and stories. It was amazing to see that common thread and common bond that twelfth house people share. Group members would feel validated and accepted by others. You begin to realize that everyone in the twelfth house group is very similar in personality, temperament and interests. The Neptunian energy is heightened when you have twelfth house planets and there is a spiritual feeling in that group that brings many people peace.

One thing that helped me, that we talked about earlier, is the gift of time. You also have to accept that most people are not like you. Most people are not going to be as kind, forgiving and compassionate as you. They are not going to be able to love you unconditionally as you do for them. You need to accept this fact and realize it's true. Take off the rose-colored glasses and start seeing people clearly. Accept that other people can never love as strongly, and unconditionally as you do! Repeat this three times. Let it sink in. You love in a very deep, mystical way and it's not your fault. You were born this way. Although sometimes it is your fault. You can cause your own pain by making these people number one in your life. You put others first and often sacrifice yourself. You have to face the reality of this pattern, and look in the mirror at yourself, and know that you are part of the problem too. The universe is not out to get you. You are not being punished, although there were many times I felt that way. I questioned, "God, how could you do this to me!" As time went by, I realized I was not seeing things clearly. I was romanticizing everything. Stinking Neptune! The cloud, the fog, the illusion, the secrets, all come out later.

You have to stop putting all these other people first, and start putting yourself first. You have to forgive. This comes easy for twelfth house people. You can forgive others very easily, but forgiving yourself is one of the hardest things to do. You will wallow and blame yourself and you will have self-pity. You might feel like you were a victim and you did something wrong. You may feel guilty and experience shame for things that were not your fault. You need to stop doing that, because it's not your fault if other people treat you badly. You cannot control how other people will treat you, but you can control how you respond to them. You just have to learn lessons of the twelfth house and how it brings you face to face with your past karma.

It is a lesson to be learned and karma makes you stronger, tougher and makes you a well-rounded person. Things happen in life for a reason and you have to learn to move on. You have to get up again and trust again. You have to do it with boundaries that you slowly develop along the way. You have to learn to have a little bit of a thicker skin, and learn to trust your own intuition. Listen to that inner voice inside your soul nudging you towards things or putting thoughts in your head. One of the things that helped me the most was to reassess why something happened and how I got myself into situations where I got so blindsided and hurt. Typically, it was because I never trusted my intuition from the beginning. I ignored that little voice inside my head that told me that a certain person was not nice, something seemed off, or their behavior was a red flag I ignored. Almost every time I ignored my own intuitive feelings, I have always regretted it. Twelfth house people have spiritual gifts, which we will talk about in the next chapter, and one of those is the gift of intuition. Intuition is a sense of knowing something, feeling it and believing it's true. When you ignore your intuition, you will later realize that you were right all along. Many twelfth house people tell me stories about how they always listened to their intuition about everything, except when it had to do with people they had a strong connection, passion or intimate love for. That is when they tend to ignore the red flags. If something does not feel right or something seems off, please trust yourself. I started listening to myself and it helped me heal.

We discussed in a previous chapter about your desire to spend time alone. Spending time alone helped me greatly. Just don't isolate yourself too much. Isolating enough to spend time in contemplation can help you. You need to have a healthy balance. You can heal in silence. You know twelfth house people love being alone, by themselves, doing things they want to do. You like to be alone, and when you do feel lonely, it usually comes from pain and heartbreak that you have experienced. That is where your true loneliness stems from. It also comes from feeling different from everyone else. You often feel like an outsider when you have twelfth house planets. You feel like most people would never understand you.

Sitting in silence listening to music, meditating and relaxing can all help twelfth house people heal and move forward. Journaling and writing down your emotions, thoughts, beliefs and experiences can be extremely therapeutic. It can help you find greater clarity. I find that writing helped me process my anger. It also helped me when I struggled through different stages of the grief process.

Grief researcher Elisabeth Kübler-Ross discussed the five stages of grief and these stages can help you when you are trying to heal from past loss. The stages do not always occur in order, and everyone grieves differently, and in a different way. All in all, these stages are very close to what most people will experience during the process of moving forward.

The stages are Denial, Bargaining, Anger, Depression and Acceptance. Denial is when you can't see what is happening completely and you can't face the painful emotions. Bargaining is when you question the universe and offer to do things differently if only you can have your lover back or change the past. Anger is when you start to realize things are not going to be like they were and underneath the anger is usually sadness. Depression occurs when you feel you have lost hope for change and you start to realize you will not be able to go back to the way it used to be. This can be a sad realization. You can feel anxiety, and depression, have difficulty sleeping and might struggle with substances to cope. I feel the anger phase is often the most difficult for twelfth house people. Through my research, I find that most twelfth house people are very uncomfortable with being angry, showing anger, feeling anger or even admitting they are angry. It is hard for you to acknowledge anger, because you might feel it is a negative thing.

Many twelfth house people were never taught how to express anger in a healthy way or how to communicate unpleasant feelings. Twelfth house people often learn to stuff their anger deep down inside and even deny it. You might even feel it's wrong to ever be angry at anyone. You might be on a mission to eradicate anger from your life and never even allow yourself to feel the emotion of anger. I had to learn that it was normal to feel angry and there was nothing wrong with feeling that way. You have every right to feel angry when someone hurts, betrays or lies to you. The first step is to get comfortable with the emotion of anger and change your attitude about it. Journaling is a good way to express your anger in a positive way.

Another thing that can help you move forward is exercise. Exercise can really help when you are healing from heartbreak. It can be hard to get motivated to do it, especially when you are hurting and not feeling good. If you don't feel like running or going to the gym, you can just walk. Just go on a walk, but do some cardio where you sweat and get your heart rate up. I don't know if it will help you, but it always helps me.

Learning how to take time for self-care is important. If you learn to take care of yourself and learn to say no to social outings when you really need time alone, you develop boundaries naturally. Practicing self-care includes spending time alone, walking, reading, listening to music, hanging out with friends, going shopping and all those other things you like to do. Whatever it is, you need to do things for yourself. Other things that might help you heal are getting a massage and energy healing such as Reiki or healing touch therapies with a certified energy healer who can actually help you move negative energy out of your body. You can pursue a lot of alternative medical techniques to heal your mind, body and spirit.

Twelfth house people often share an experience where the pain you feel is felt physically inside your body, often the heart area. You can experience chest pain, and a strange weight inside your chest, often in the heart chakra area. I believe in the chakras, which are energy centers in the body, and when you are heartbroken you can feel it physically. They say that you can die from a broken heart. I actually believe that might be true. It feels like a knife is stuck in your chest. Sometimes you feel it on your back and it goes straight through your heart. It aches and physically hurts. I don't wish that pain on anyone, but as a twelfth house person you have to go through heartbreak. Often you are hurt by the ones that you love the most. Many people with twelfth house planets have shared these experiences with me. One of the most helpful ways to heal twelfth house energy is self-care and self-awareness. Twelfth house people are experts at helping other people heal. You can research self-care online and find lots of great resources that might be beneficial. I recommend focusing on your health, self-care techniques that we discussed, and self-reflection. Sometimes it takes time, and small steps towards changing your habits.

Twelfth house people love deeply and connect with others easily. You care too much sometimes, which is your blessing and curse. You have to realize the reality that sometimes people do not love you back. That reality can be hard, and takes time to remember. Many people are incapable of loving other people like you love them. You will be disappointed by people time and time again, until you accept the truth that this will happen. Helping other people can also help you heal from heartbreak. Serving other people and helping them is the key mission of twelfth house people. You will be good at helping others who have experienced heartbreak because you can empathize with how others truly feel.

You are meant to be strong and brave. You should not let how other people treat you change who you are, and never lose your loving, kind and compassionate nature. Remember that you are meant to be an angel. Do not let the past heartache change you into someone you're not. You have to try to truly let things go and do whatever you have to for you to heal. Sometimes I think the hardest part of letting go and healing from heartbreak is your mind and thoughts. It is natural to over-analyze things and overthink about what happened. Overthinking and obsessing on the memories can make things worse. Do not get caught in that trap. Let things go the best you can and forgive yourself. Learn to love yourself as much as you loved that other person.

It will be different for each person, and some things work

better for some than others. It could take you more time and effort to forgive than someone else. I find that most twelfth house people forgive others easily, but find it difficult to forgive themselves for the mistakes they made. You might feel lonely, but remember that you are never alone. You can always reach out to someone for help or to talk to. You might feel that your family and friends do not understand you, or how much you hurt. Other twelfth house people will understand you, and you can always post in my twelfth house astrology Facebook group and reach out. Someone will answer you and help you. Even when you feel no one else is there for you when you need them, you are not alone.

You have to look within yourself and become your own soul mate. That is the destiny of a twelfth house person. You are being molded and changed into a spiritual being. You are not just a physical body and you are aware of that fact. Becoming spiritual and connecting with God, Source, or a higher power is the mission of a twelfth house person. Through experiencing pain and heartache you naturally become more spiritual. Heartbreak can lead you to seek a connection with God and a connection with others. If you never experience pain or loss, it is going to be a little harder to truly seek oneness with the divine or whatever religion or belief system that you follow. Many people with twelfth house planets have shared with me similar stories of seeking God. All twelfth house people have similar lessons to learn, personality traits, experiences, gifts and similar painful challenges. You are meant to rise up, so you can accomplish your very important mission of helping others and expressing your gifts to the world.

Having strong boundaries and protecting yourself will only help you in the future. Many twelfth house people share with me that they were shocked by many things that happened to them. They feel that they have experienced trauma. It is sometimes hard for you to believe that certain things actually happened to you. Sometimes you regret not listening to your inner voice, because you were intuitive from the beginning. Many twelfth house people dream things that warn them of the future. This happened to me several times, and I learned this lesson the hard way. I believed that a dream I had was showing me the future when really it was a warning. I misinterpreted the dream and made life choices based on it. Twelfth house people need to be careful of taking your dreams as one hundred percent true; they are just signals. Forgive yourself and let it go. Your dreams are a gift to you and are a huge part of your life. I can't imagine not being able to dream.

There are some people that you will have better life connections and soul connections with. There is really no such thing as true love and a soul mate. You have past connections with certain people and karmic learning that you have to balance out. Twelfth house people are here to balance out karma with many people, so you can pursue a spiritual path this lifetime. You have to learn to be more realistic and down to earth about love. This will help you prevent experiencing heartbreak over and over again. Time heals all wounds and as more time goes by you will reflect and realize that you learned many valuable lessons about yourself, others and life.

Chapter Six

Spiritual Abilities & Mystical Experiences

I dream of the future. When I sleep I look forward to what dreams my soul gives me as I slumber. The images are deep and vivid. My dreams guide my life and prepare me for karma coming into my life.
– A.D., Ohio

As a twelfth house person you are someone who is born with spiritual abilities and psychic gifts. You often inherit these gifts from your mother, father or from someone on their side of the family such as a grandparent. For me, it was my maternal grandmother who passed along to me her gift of dreaming about the future. My grandmother was also very intuitive. She is the only person I have ever met who actually saw an angel. My grandmother had the Sun in the twelfth house, so it was no surprise that she was blessed with spiritual gifts. I never knew that she was like me until I was 19. My grandfather would tell me that she would wake him up in the middle of the night, telling him that she had a bad dream. Then he said, the exact thing she dreamed would happen. He was a little scared to even talk about it, but they were married for over 60 years, so I am sure he heard a lot of her dreams.

The day she told me that she saw an angel, I believed her. She told me she went to take a nap in the guest room, which she often did daily in the afternoon. She said she woke up and saw a purple mist around the ceiling of the room. She knew she was awake when she saw someone standing at the side of her bed. She looked closely and it was a woman. She then heard the words, "Everything is going to be okay." After she heard these words, she watched the woman turn and walk away. When she watched her walk away, the woman had huge brownish wings.

She watched her walk into the wall and vanish. Right after this visitation, my grandfather got very sick. My grandmother had to be his caretaker for over a year due to a back injury. Things did get better, but the message was to prepare her. I find that twelfth house people often get messages from angels, spirit guides and loved ones who have crossed over to the other side. You have that support of guardians watching over you when you have planets in the twelfth house.

There are many spiritual gifts that twelfth house people are blessed with. I am going to focus on a few of the most common gifts that I have found in my own life, and in the lives of clients who have shared their stories with me. We are going to look at mystical, unexplained experiences such as dreams, clairvoyance and intuition.

Mystical Experiences

Many twelfth house people have mystical experiences. These are experiences that are hard to explain to anyone, because they are so different and special. Mystical experiences often involve something otherworldly, or something that is not a normal day-to-day event. Some examples might be waking up in the middle of the night and seeing someone standing at the foot of your bed. Many twelfth house people are extremely spiritual and open to spirits. They wake up in the night seeing deceased loved ones. I understand why this happens to many twelfth house people when they are children. It is because of the Neptune energy that rules this house.

I started researching many different things, and learned a lot about the tree of life. For the first time in my life, it made sense to me how some people can see spirits upon falling asleep or waking up. As humans we live in the earth realm, which is known as Malkuth. This is the lowest realm on the tree of life. Yesod is the closest realm to earth and is the astral realm. The astral realm is like a veil in our world. Those with spiritual sensitivities can see and feel things that are in that realm. It explains how my grandmother saw the angel and many other experiences that I will share in this chapter.

Mystical experiences to me are unexplained experiences. They are beyond the practical world. These experiences can be difficult to describe and even share with others, because we often feel that no one will believe us. I find that twelfth house energy enhances these experiences. These experiences are destined for you to have so that you can continue your journey as a spiritual healer. These experiences are something that is unique to twelfth house people. In my twelfth house astrology group on Facebook, I am always validated by shared posts about different topics such as dreams, mystical experiences and unexplained intuition. For the first time in my life, I read about exact experiences that I have had. I see firsthand that many people with twelfth house planets are the same and share similar mystical experiences.

When you have twelfth house planets you are gifted with spiritual vision. I used to think I was alone in this world until I started reading about all the members' experiences in my group. They were all similar. People from all over the world with twelfth house planets come together to connect and help each other.

A common unexplained experience is one where you see glowing orbs of light. Many twelfth house people have shared with me how they have seen these glowing orbs at different times in their lives. When I was a teenager, I had an experience with a glowing orb of light. I don't talk about it as much now that I am in my 40s, but my entire life was changed by that experience. I remember waking up in my bedroom in the middle of the night after a basketball game. I had a really good game that night and was 16 years old. I was actually trying to get scholarships and recruited for playing basketball. I remember that my dad and brother were on a fishing trip, so my mother and I were alone in the house. We had a small home and my parents' bedroom was right across the hall from me. I was always afraid of the dark when I was younger. I had to have a night light on or my door wide open with a night light in the bathroom to sleep at night. I had to have my bed facing the door so I could see out. I never enjoyed sleeping as a young person, because I would either have vivid, life-like dreams, sleepwalk and be woken up by my parents, or I would wake up in my dreams and be mentally aware that I was dreaming.

This night in particular, I woke up and looked towards my doorway. I saw a glowing ball of light floating in the doorway. I could not move and I was laying on my back frozen. I tried to scream for my mother, but I had no voice. Whatever this was, it had a hold of me. It is something I can't explain in words. At that time, I was afraid of the unknown and I was not sure what it was. It was about the size of a softball, and was a translucent, watery shape orb floating there. I realized that the only thing that I could control was my mind. I kept praying for it not to come inside my room and I laid there watching it for hours.

After laying frozen and paranoid watching it float in my doorway, it would leave and then come right back. At some point during this experience, I got my voice back. I screamed out for my mother. She heard me, and I told her to look in my doorway. I asked her if she saw the light in my doorway and she yelled back, "Yes." I asked her to get up and see what it was. She started rationalizing it like a normal person would. She told me that maybe it was a flashlight that someone was shining in the window. I yelled, "No, it moves and it has a watery form." She then said maybe it's a lightning bug. I begged her to get up, but she told me to go back to sleep. I continued to lay there until I finally passed out. The next morning my mother told me that it was definitely not a lightning bug. She admitted that she had no idea what it was. She seemed a little scared about it and I was too. That experience started me on my search of spiritual things such as spirits and angels. This was the year I found astrology. I bought my first astrology book and began teaching myself. For the first time in my life, I felt validated when I read about the Sun in the twelfth house. It explained why I had these strange experiences that no one else had. I knew there was something different about my personality and feelings. This experience got me on the path of wanting to understand myself and others better.

When planets are placed in the twelfth house, you are someone who is going to seek answers to the meaning of life. Many times you begin seeking answers because of the mystical experiences that you had as a child and young adult. Your experiences often start at a young age. Many twelfth house people tell me they do not really remember being a child. They hear stories about how they talked to the air and no one was there, played with imaginary friends, and would wake up their parents in the night because of a vivid dream. Sometimes you saw grandma at the foot of your bed. How do you explain that to someone? It is one of the reasons twelfth house people feel lonely until they find their tribe and meet other like-minded people who understand and accept them.

You need to trust yourself. You need to embrace the strange and unexplained experiences you have. Many twelfth house people share with me that they did not always have parents or family who nurtured their natural spiritual gifts. This causes many twelfth house people to doubt and push down their natural spiritual abilities. You are connected to spirit, and you are born with natural psychic abilities. These things that you experience are a part of you and natural to you. As children you are often told that it is just your imagination and you begin to doubt your own special mystical experiences. You were born with these gifts to help others and to help yourself in this journey.

When planets are placed in the twelfth house, your energy is wide open. A common experience that many twelfth house people have is that you disconnect from your body. Some people call this astral projection. One client shared with me that she could not fall asleep at night and had difficulties. At night she would leave her body. I asked her to describe to me what happened. She explained that as she relaxed and drifted off into her subconscious her astral body would leave. She would be looking down at herself lying in the bed. This happened throughout her life, and was a difficult experience for her because her family did not know how to support her. They had no knowledge of this type of experience.

A friend of mine who has the Sun in the twelfth house shared similar experiences with leaving her body. She started leaving her body when she would meditate. It would also happen when she was trying to fall asleep at night. Another twelfth house client shared with me that she was in a car accident when she was 16 years old. She was clinically dead for 20 minutes. They revived her and she was in the hospital for a long time. After that experience, she had difficulty sleeping because she would leave her body and float above it. She became addicted to sleep medication and other medical drugs to cope. One theory I have about this is that possibly the silver cord that attaches us to our body was severed when she was in the car accident. She had no control of this experience and it frightened her. Plus she could never get a good night sleep and her health was being affected. I did some research on the silver cord and the astral body after talking with her. I still believe that it might have been the reason she left her body without trying to do so when she tried to sleep.

Other clients share with me that they want to astral project and leave the body, similar to what Buddhist monks do. I have watched a lot of movies and the one movie I think about is *Ace Ventura: When Nature Calls* with Jim Carrey. I laughed hard at the part where he meditated and left his body. I do believe that highly spiritual people have the ability to astral project and even control it. There are many documented stories about this experience. The reason I share it here is to validate twelfth house people's unique experiences. These are things that science, as of yet, cannot explain rationally. We have no scientific way to disprove these experiences or prove them. I think the mystical and unexplained energy of the twelfth house enhances these experiences. Just because no one else understands does not mean that your experiences are not real. I always used to say that if I see it, then I will believe it. I wanted to have my own spiritual experiences and that is what made it real for me. Through my own mystical experiences, I developed a stronger sense of purpose. I began to see that there is more to our physical world than meets the eye. You should not have to try to convince anyone that your experiences are real. You are the one who experienced them, and you know what you experienced even if other people do not believe you.

Other common unexplained experiences that you might have are intuitive feelings, and empathic abilities that are often accurate. You may sense that something might happen and have a feeling about it, then it happens in real life. You might feel someone's energy and know that they are struggling. When you reach out to them, you find out that they are having a hard time. You just have a feeling about things and people that is accurate. You can call it a sixth sense or gut feeling. The amazing thing is that your gut instincts are typically correct. I find that many twelfth house people learn to listen to that small voice within because it never leads them astray. The more unexplained experiences you have with your intuitive abilities, the more you begin to trust yourself. I always say that when I ignore my intuition, I get into trouble. I could have avoided so many problems in life, whether it be with relationships, people or work situations, if I had listened to that gut instinct. You are learning to trust that intuition and inner knowing that you are born with.

Dreams

The most amazing gift that twelfth house people have is the ability to have deep dreams. The twelfth house rules the subconscious mind. This is a very important part of healing. You need good sleep to rest the mind each night. When you sleep, you enter another realm known as the subconscious. Dreams are a way for twelfth house people to gather intuitive messages and information about your day-to-day life and often help you prepare for the future.

My own twelfth house experience with dreams has led me to create a dream analysis group on Facebook with the goal of helping others understand their dreams and soul messages. They say an "unexamined dream is like an unopened letter". There is so much deeper information and energy hidden behind the symbols in your dreams if you just take the time to pay attention and try to analyze them. It is important for twelfth house people to learn more about dreamwork. Dreamwork will come naturally to you and is an excellent tool for building self-awareness. I recommend getting a dream log or journal, to sit at the side of your bed with a pen. Every night you can write the date. You will prepare your subconscious mind to pay attention to your dreams. You can jot down whatever you can remember prior to completely waking up. You will find when you first wake up that your dreams are fresh in your mind. The sooner you write them down, the more you will remember what happened. If you wait too long, you will slowly forget.

As a twelfth house person, you will dream deeply and vividly. I can honestly say I have never met anyone with twelfth house planets who did not have an active dream world. I think the only planet placement in the twelfth house that I have seen that blocks dreams would be Saturn. My husband has Saturn in the twelfth and he rarely dreams. Every client I have worked with who had planets in the twelfth shared stories of a vivid dream life and said they often dreamed of future events.

Dreams are a way for your spirit to speak to you and prepare you for the future. Dreams are signals of the potential energies and reveal life situations that may happen in your life. They say that nothing ever happens in the real world until it happens in a dream. Dreaming is something that twelfth house people do best. You dream deeply and vividly, often in color. You can experience lucid dreaming where you wake up inside the dream and realize you are dreaming. This has happened to me several times in my life.

The most recent lucid dream I had occurred last year. I was flying over the beautiful blue ocean. I was flying fast over the ocean below. I looked out in the distance and I saw dolphins jumping up out of the water ahead of me. I also saw a bridge in the distance that went across the ocean. I realized I was awake. I became aware mentally that I was dreaming. That is when I started to panic, because I started waking up in the dream. I began losing control of flying and started getting closer to the water. I was awake and realized I was dreaming. I became afraid of falling into the ocean water, so I flew to the right to the land I saw. It was green and full of beautiful flowers. After I landed on the green grass I woke up.

Many twelfth house people have shared with me a strange experience that happens right as they fall asleep or as they are waking up from sleep. One client shared with me that she would have an experience where she would wake up and know she was awake lying in her bed. Suddenly, she would look and she would see someone standing there. She would realize that she was awake, and she would be unable to move so she would scream. After screaming she would be fully awake in her bed. The experience was very real to her and she was awake mentally, but not physically.

I have had this happen to me several times. I think that twelfth house people are very connected to the subconscious level. You often dream deeply and have an ability to receive information. Many twelfth house people have amazing dreams that involve angels, animals, religious figures and nature. Many dreams of twelfth house people have been signals of future events. You might dream of things before they happen. Sometimes your dreams happen years in advance and play out in the real world. It is important that you write your dreams down so you can remember them. Dream interpretation books will be helpful for you to delve deeper and find out the hidden meaning of your dream symbols. There are many dream resources and books that would help you understand the symbols.

When I studied dream interpretation, I was amazed and took a few classes about dream symbols to build on my knowledge. One of the most common symbols twelfth house people share with me is dreaming about water, specifically the ocean. It is not surprising that you often dream of water, because it symbolizes spirituality and emotions. Animals are also very common in dreams and can represent a message to you depending on which animal it is. Animals also represent habits in your life and are showing you more about something that is happening in your life.

I have dreamed enough now to know the difference between a psychic dream and a symbolic dream. I always know a dream is important or warning me of something that might actually happen in the future by the way I feel when I wake up. Other twelfth house people have shared similar experiences with me. Many twelfth house people have dreams of flying, and this might be a common dream symbol for you.

The important thing to remember about your dreaming gift is that you take the time to analyze your dreams. I think sometimes you are meant to help other people and you are given a glimpse of future events. I used to think I was the only person who dreamed things that happened until I started connecting with other people who had twelfth house planets. You will have many dreams that change your life and will realize dreaming is your gift. One thing I realize is that as you get older you might not dream as deeply and as often. I find that the most vivid dreams occur for many people during certain phases of the Moon. I find I dream most deeply and in more detail when the Moon is in a water sign such as Scorpio, Cancer or Pisces. I started noticing a pattern in my own life. I hear similar experiences from clients and you might notice this in your own life.

Having planets in the twelfth house blesses you with an ability of delving deep when you are in the dream world. You might be a dream walker or dream traveler. You might be a lucid dreamer and wake up mentally when you are still dreaming. You might be able to control and change the course of your dreams. You may sleepwalk and act out your dreams, which is another twelfth house shared experience. The key is to take your dreams seriously and pay attention to them. Always remember that dreams are signals for what is coming into your life or the lives of those around you. You can learn to use this spiritual gift to help others in a deep way.

Intuition

Twelfth house people are born with a sixth sense and inner knowing about many things. Your greatest gift is your ability to feel and sense what is going on with people around you. You are sensitive to energy and connect with others on a deeper level. Your gut instincts are always right and you need to listen to that small voice within. You often learn the hard way that your intuition is there to protect you. The more you work on trusting yourself, the more people you can help.

The gift of intuition is often inherited. You might find that a parent or a grandparent shares this same gift with you.

Many twelfth house people share with me that there was often a grandparent who had spiritual abilities such as intuition and clairvoyance who helped guide them. The twelfth house represents karma from your past. You often reconnect with people where the karma needs to be balanced. This is why it's important to listen to your intuitive nature as you walk through life. It will help you when you feel challenged in life. It will help you listen to your inner voice before you make decisions. The more you balance your mind, body and spirit, the more you will tap into your intuitive gifts.

Energy Healing

Many twelfth house people sense energy. Energy surrounds everyone and everything. When you have planets placed in the twelfth house you often are drawn to career fields associated with healing. Many twelfth house people share with me their interest in Reiki energy healing techniques, Pranic Healing and various alternative healing practices involving crystals. I was always attracted to these spiritual techniques and took Reiki certification courses. I enjoy learning more about all of these modalities. I believe that healing takes place on the mental, emotional and physical levels. There is so much more that we don't know scientifically about how the physical body heals. Trauma researchers have associated unhealed emotional pain and wounds with increased risk of illness. I have witnessed this throughout my life, while working with trauma victims. The connection between the emotions and the manifestation of illness has been well researched.

You are a natural healer. You can feel the heat of the energy coming from your hands. You might also sense where other people's energy is blocked in their aura field and chakras. Chakras are the energy centers that are associated with each major gland in the body. Even if you have not studied energy healing techniques, you will be attracted to helping others heal.

This is one tool that I find many twelfth house people study to increase their ability to help others.

All twelfth house people have spiritual gifts and mystical experiences sometime in their lives. I have never met anyone with planets in the twelfth house that have not shared with me personal experiences of unexplained coincidences, intuitive knowing, dreams of the future and other amazing phenomenon. Most of these experiences are very personal in nature and hard to explain to people. Just remember it is a blessing of the twelfth house to experience these amazing things. Always remember that you are not alone. Many people with twelfth house planets would understand you perfectly, and they would believe you. Do not doubt your own personal spiritual experiences. The experiences that you have are meant to be. You are meant to see things that others do not see. You are meant to feel things others do not feel. You see through the veil into another world and see deeper into all of life's mysteries.

Chapter Seven

Addiction & Coping Skills

I had an absent father figure. I have a Leo Sun in the 12th house. Even before I knew anything about this placement, I decided to stop drinking for two reasons. First, because of my father's drinking problems. Secondly, because drinking leads me into depression. I decided to stay away from alcohol. I am focusing on being the best version of me. I feel that meditation is the best way to be in contact with the deepest parts of me without having all the negatives of substance use.
– S.R., California

The twelfth house is often associated with addiction. The planet Neptune rules the twelfth house and the sign Pisces. All of these energies and traits increase your need to escape. Sometimes addiction is something twelfth house people experience themselves or with other people in their lives. I often find that when you have personal planets in the twelfth house, such as the Sun and Moon, you may be drawn to escape from the pain you feel by trying to numb yourself. Part of the reason you do this is because you are very sensitive. I also find that many times you will experience family addiction. Often your father or mother might struggle with addiction in some form. You can find it difficult to express yourself at times so drinking alcohol is often the drug of choice, because it relaxes you. Sometimes twelfth house people like the feeling that alcohol gives them. It loosens your inhibitions.

Sleep can also become an addiction for twelfth house people. I find that sleeping has always been something that helped me heal. I also realize it was something that I did when I was feeling sad or depressed. I remember I used to sleep in on the weekends until noon, and stay up late. I was always a night owl but that is hard to do when you have a job where you have to be at work before seven in the morning. I always loved to sleep in and dream. My dreams would be vivid, and the longer I slept in, the more dreams I had. I would wake up in the morning and write them down in my dream log and date them. I started doing this in high school.

A lot of twelfth house people tell me that they like to sleep their life away. I used to joke that I loved to sleep when I was younger. I craved sleep and actually used to look forward to going to bed every night so I could have dreams. Sleeping can be a way to escape and become an unhealthy coping mechanism and addiction. If you have twelfth house planets you will enjoy sleeping when you get stressed. There is a fine line between being addicted to something and abusing things. Some people abuse food by overeating and indulging in negative eating habits. You might eat to numb your negative emotions or overeat during stressful times. You may also abuse your body by overdoing it and exercising too much. There is a difference between abuse and addiction. Addiction means that your habits become a crutch and it's something that you have difficulty giving up. If you don't do it then you can find things a little bit difficult. It might be hard to focus on completing tasks and functioning with a routine.

Other addictive behaviors you might have could be exercising, sex, food, work and anything that becomes a compulsion. Food addiction and electronic cell phone addiction are more well known today. You know when you eat chocolate or sugar it creates the feel-good chemical in your brain. It increases endorphins which are connected to addicting behaviors. You get addicted to things because they feel good at the moment. It fulfills you and makes your brain feel emotionally better. It is like a quick fix. Many people get addicted to different things because they temporarily relieve stress. I have known twelfth house people who become workaholics. I am guilty of this myself. You can become driven and pursue work with strong passion ignoring your own emotions and your own health. Sometimes twelfth house people avoid going within and feeling because it can be painful. Sometimes it is easier to ignore what you are feeling and suppress it. Twelfth house people are good at pretending that everything is fine emotionally, even if you are falling apart inside. Internet addiction is also another way that people zone out and cope with the world. It can become a crutch and a way to avoid living in the real world. There is a lot of research being done about Internet use and screen time. There is proof that it can affect your relationships, sleep, mood and brain chemistry.

You feel so many emotions and energies in your environment that you sometimes need to escape. The important thing to learn is that you have the potential to become dependent. You might use these negative things as a coping mechanism and crutch. As a twelfth house person you can be more prone to addiction than other people. It is important to be aware of this trait inside yourself and understand your own personality and coping mechanisms.

Many twelfth house people tell me that they experience addiction to feeling love and intense emotions. Love addiction is a real thing that can make you feel obsessed and out of control. You might find it hard to let people go. You can also become obsessed with spirituality and escape through meditation. You can do many things to the extreme and become imbalanced. The goal is to try to balance these behaviors and habits.

When I worked as a social worker years ago, I started looking at the charts of clients that shared with me that they were in twelve step programs for alcohol addiction. I began to research certain placements in their charts and found that many of these clients had the Sun placed in the twelfth house. I also found through my research that a predominant amount of them had

Pisces energy, specifically the Sun in Pisces. I dug a little deeper and collected more data. I found the Moon as well as Pluto in the twelfth in those who had struggled with addiction. I began to believe that any planet in the twelfth house could affect this energy and increase your desire to want to escape from painful emotions and experiences. The most relevant planet I found that impacted addictive tendencies was Neptune. I found that many twelfth house people also had Neptune in the first house or conjunct the ascendent.

Twelfth house people's desire to escape from the world through substances can lead to self-abuse and you can hurt yourself. If you abuse alcohol or other substances your behaviors might affect other people. You often hurt yourself the most. I find that twelfth house addictions tend to be focused inward and that you hurt yourself before you hurt others. An example is drinking until you pass out. This affects you directly. Whereas when I researched the eighth house, I found that eighth house people's addictions tend to be focused more on dramatic situations that affect other people. This is just my opinion of what I have seen throughout the years. I have seen that twelfth house people tend to hurt themselves through addictions due to a need to escape. You don't like to hurt other people and do your best to avoid that at all costs.

As a twelfth house person, you are very sensitive and kind. You could not bear to know that your behavior hurt other people. You might be blind to this fact. The Neptune energy that rules the twelfth house affects how you see things. You can have a fog surrounding you that blinds you and you can't see your own problems or addictions. You may not truly know you have a problem, even if other people notice it. If you know that you have family members that suffered with addiction, you could also be predisposed genetically to addictive behaviors. For instance if a parent or grandparent had alcoholism, this is something that you should be aware of and think about so you can develop healthy coping skills.

I find a lot of people with twelfth house planets smoke cigarettes. Many psychics and empaths smoke. I might be generalizing here but I have been to many psychic fairs and met many different healers and they all admitted they smoke. The two most intuitive people I have ever met both smoke and are unable to quit. They both have twelfth house Sun and are very psychic. I remember telling my friend who is very psychic how bad smoking cigarettes was for her. I am a Virgo so I have always disliked cigarette smoke. My friend is a twelfth house Sun. When I told her she should quit smoking, she told me that it was the only thing that helped her cope and survive. She asked me to please not take her cigarettes from her and she got very upset. After that day, I accepted that she is going to smoke. She needed it to cope with her intense emotions. Is she addicted to smoking? Maybe. It's probably not the most healthy thing to do, but for her it's important for her survival in this world. If it makes her happier and able to function, then who am I to judge.

Twelfth house people need to find what works for them and what things help them bounce back. If it is a glass of wine every night, so be it. If it's smoking a few cigarettes before you go into a mental health clinic to listen to people's problems all day, then do it. I think problems arise for twelfth house people when alcohol is involved. I find that alcohol is typically something that can be more damaging to twelfth house people than other substances. There is a saying to drink when you are merry. I think that is a spiritual message. Alcohol is a depressant. You may drink to relax or to help you sleep. When you drink and you are already struggling with depression, you might get more depressed creating a vicious cycle.

I think a good motto for twelfth house people is to drink when you are happy and try to be cautious about drinking too much when you are stressed, depressed, angry or having relationship problems. There are other things that you can do to express your unpleasant emotions like writing, journaling, meditation, exercise, prayer, reading, travel and many more things that might work for you. Everyone benefits from different activities but primarily twelfth house people benefit from solitary activities and time alone.

Chapter Eight

Secrets & Illusions

I never knew my grandmother was like me. I did not find out until I was in college that she dreamed things that happened, just like me. It was kind of a family secret and no one ever talked about it. I always thought I was the oddball in the family and felt so alone. It was a relief to hear my grandmother believed me and she had dreams of the future that happened too.
– J.T., Ohio

The twelfth house hides behind a veil of illusion. Illusion makes it difficult for twelfth house people to see clearly. You walk in two worlds and have one foot in each realm. You are connected to spirit, but find yourself stuck in this material plane. You are here but do not feel like you belong here, because your heart is in the spiritual realms. The secret energy of the twelfth house is something that many people are afraid of. I remember reading astrology books when I was younger, in the 1990s, and most books at that time had a negative interpretation of the twelfth house. There are better twelfth house books out there now that are more positive, but in the old days, our ancestors were afraid of the twelfth house. I think the main reason this fear existed is because of the natural mysterious and invisible energy that this house creates.

It is hard for someone without twelfth house planets to fully understand it or explain it. When we talk about secrets in the astrological chart we often look to the twelfth and eighth houses. I find that both houses rule secret things. The twelfth house specifically has a different energy and interpretation of secrets than the eighth house. Planets in the twelfth house manifest differently. When planets are placed in the twelfth house, the energy of the planet is kept repressed and hidden from you. There is so much about yourself that you do not even know, or realize because you have never seen it or felt it.

Twelfth house secrets are truly a part of who you are and can affect many things in your life such as your parents, family, friends and relationships. All of these things have energy that is hidden or kept from you in some way. Sometimes these secrets are things that other people know, but due to your twelfth house energy you never even notice them. For example, your father may be an alcoholic and you never knew that. You sometimes noticed that he acted strange and withdrawn, but you never saw him drinking alcohol. When you grew up, you eventually realized it and saw it more clearly. The illusions surrounding the secrets are lifted and the fog slowly fades away.

The twelfth house secrets are things you will never know or will not realize until later in life. The energy creates a mist or fog around certain areas of your life. The secrets surrounding your life and those closest to you are never revealed fully. Even if you suspect something, it feels like there is no closure or truth revealed.

I will briefly discuss planets in the twelfth house and how they create secrecy and repressed energy in your life. If the Sun is placed in the twelfth house then your main identity and who you are is kept hidden. You may feel that you like to hide from the world and do not like being the center of attention or being noticed. You also can have a deep feeling that you do not truly know your own self. It sometimes feels like there is a huge part of you that is hiding behind a screen. You try to reach these parts of yourself, but have difficulty connecting to them. The Sun also represents the father figure in your life. When the Sun is in the twelfth house in the natal chart, there are many secrets surrounding your father and things about him you might not know. Secrets can be many things and you truly are not aware of them while growing up.

The father figure energy might be missing from your life. Some twelfth house people tell me that they never had a connection to their father. You felt an absent or missing bond with your father. If you felt an absent bond with your father, this is a common experience with this placement. I wrote an article years ago called, "The Sun in the Twelfth House: Suffering & the Father," to try to help twelfth house people understand the karmic learning of this placement.

When the Moon is placed in the twelfth house, you are a person who keeps your emotions hidden and secret. You might have difficulty expressing what you feel because you are not really sure yourself. Your emotions and reactions are deep and intense. Your emotions might be strong, but you do not like to openly share them with others unless you fully trust them. The Moon in your chart represents the mother figure in your life. When the Moon is placed in the twelfth house, there might be things about your mother that you do not see or know. You might find your mother to be spiritual and emotionally unstable. Sometimes when the Moon is in the twelfth house your mother seems mysterious and unreachable in some way. You might have difficulty connecting with her or you might be very attached to her and take care of her in some way.

When Mercury is placed in the twelfth house, you might find it difficult to express your true thoughts. Your thoughts are deep and you often keep them secret. Sometimes you feel that you do not know how to express what you think, and your mind is blocked from expressing your ideas. You might benefit from writing and journaling, so you can express your true thoughts openly. You might feel that you have much to say but when you get ready to say something it's like you forget the words. You have a creative mind and are born with intuitive knowledge. You probably have an interest in studying metaphysical and new age topics such as astrology, tarot, meditation, and anything that is spiritual and unique.

When Mars is placed in the twelfth house your anger and passion can be watered down. There might be times that you are not even aware that you are upset or angry. Having Mars in the twelfth house can create a secretive nature concerning conflict. You might not feel comfortable expressing your anger outwardly and you can turn it inwardly on yourself. It is important that you learn to connect with your passion and intense feelings so you do not repress and get sick. You need a good balance in your life to express yourself. Exercise might help such as walking or hiking outdoors.

When Venus is placed in the twelfth house, your emotions and feelings are kept hidden. You might have a very secretive love nature and keep your true feelings to yourself. You hide your love from others due to shyness, and an inability to understand how to express your intense love nature. You could experience secret or hidden love affairs that no one ever knows about. You are also born with artistic and creative talents that you might practice in secret in the comfort of your own home. You will benefit by expressing your loving feelings through writing, journaling, music and creative arts.

When Jupiter is placed in the twelfth house you might keep your energy secret and hidden. Jupiter is the planet of abundance, expression and good luck. You do not like to stand out and even when good things happen in your life, so you might keep those things private. You will benefit from unseen forces and it's like guardian angels are watching out for you behind the scenes. You will also benefit by expressing your creative nature through private pursuits where you can feel peaceful and comfortable.

When Saturn is placed in the twelfth house, you might feel restricted in expressing yourself. The secrets that you keep have to do with your feelings of sadness and depression. You do not openly let people know when you are struggling. You may fight hard to hide many things about yourself. You have a seriousness about you and might have fears surrounding being open and expressing your artistic abilities. You can also be very disciplined and responsible feeling like you have to take care of others. It is important that you make time to take care of your own feelings and thoughts in order to catch yourself when you become negative. You will benefit by focusing on positive goals and working behind the scenes in secret to pursue them.

When Uranus is placed in the twelfth house you will experience flashes of insight and have unexpected psychic experiences. You will have an eccentric nature but will keep it secret from others around you. You might have unique hobbies and beliefs that you keep private and do behind the scenes. You will benefit from jotting down your unexpected insights and flashes of wisdom. You might have visions of the future and can use these abilities to help other people.

When Neptune is placed in the twelfth house, you will have deep dreams when you sleep. You will have difficulty with boundaries and feel everything in your environment. You will be extremely empathic, and will enjoy escaping from the world to spend time alone. You will be naturally secretive and keep things to yourself, as you enjoy spending time alone in your fantasy world. You might feel very detached from reality and enjoy escaping into your imagination. You will be very sensitive to your environment, and it is important that you surround yourself with healthy and positive people. Other people might perceive you as dreamy, mystical and otherworldly. You will benefit from spiritual pursuits such as energy grounding exercises, meditation, deep breathing and yoga.

When Pluto is placed in the twelfth house, you will have a very secretive nature. Other people might perceive you as intense and brooding. You might feel that people either love you or hate you. Your emotions are strong and intense, but you repress them and keep them secret. You have powerful psychic abilities and might be connected to the dead. You might keep your psychic intuition to yourself until you begin to trust your feelings. You can have a strong need to connect and bond with other people like you. You crave deep intimacy, but might keep your true feelings private. You do not trust people as easily as other twelfth house people.

Twelfth house people can be secretive and can see things as they want them to be, not as they really are, making them prone to illusions. Illusions can cloud your judgment and emotions. Sometimes you only see the good in people and this can lead to heartache. You might also not believe in yourself and your abilities. You might have illusions and fears that are not accurate. You will benefit by focusing on developing a practical and realistic approach to life. The more grounded you become, the less you will be prone to illusions. You will not be blindsided by people that take from you without giving back. You will start to see the world and other people for how they really are and accept that reality.

Chapter Nine

Service to Others, Compassion & Secret Enemies

I find that those I trust the most always hurt me or betray me. I used to think I had secret enemies. It is always someone I never thought would go against me that ends up turning on me. Now that I get older, I realize it is really my own illusion of seeing the good in everyone and never listening to my gut instinct about certain people.
– G.S., Arizona

The twelfth house is often called the house of suffering. I think this is an outdated connection that is associated with this house. It is true that twelfth house people have a special destiny and they experience loss and pain, but so does everyone. I think the main thing to remember about the energy of the twelfth house is that it is about helping others and walking a spiritual path. If you have planets in the twelfth house and focus on helping other people in some way, you will avoid much of the suffering that many astrologers talk about regarding this house.

I will agree that when planets are in the twelfth house, you have to focus on pursuing a spiritual path and greater mission as to why you are here on this earth. I think that through my research I have realized that even with the losses twelfth house people experience in life, they tell me they would never change a thing in their natal chart. When asked, they tell me they would keep all their twelfth house placements. The main thing that many twelfth house people share with me is that they have had so many spiritual and mystical experiences that confirmed to them that there is a higher power that they would not change a thing. Through experience, you develop an inner knowing, and a belief in karma and that everything happens for a reason. Even when the universe strips things away from you, you will continue pursuing the path of the servant. Helping others comes naturally to twelfth house people, and by helping others you also help yourself in the process.

Twelfth house energy pushes us to serve, and when we focus on our higher calling and lofty mission of helping others who need support, we attract many blessings. Many positive things and experiences can come into your life when you allow yourself to truly serve others. The goal of service is to fulfill your mission here on earth and twelfth house people are here for a greater purpose—that is why you chose to be born with twelfth house planets. I find comfort in knowing that I chose my chart and my soul knew the exact set of circumstances needed for my future growth. You are here to learn spiritual lessons and increase soul knowledge. The purpose of life is not to work, pay bills and then die. Twelfth house people simply can't live a life that narrow. They know there is something much greater out there and they have a deep desire to connect with it.

Twelfth house people are born with compassion. Compassion is the ability to recognize suffering in others and take action to help. Twelfth house people are born to do this. You sense and feel when someone needs help and sometimes you do not have to do anything because people who need healing will find you. You naturally attract those who need compassion and are gifted at giving it selflessly.

Some twelfth house people tell me they always wear their heart on their sleeve. You might feel that you are vulnerable because you are too nice and giving. You are meant to be giving and compassionate, and that is your strength. Never change this part of you. The world needs you to serve and show compassion because many people do not know how to do that. You are born to do that and it is part of your spiritual mission.

The twelfth house is associated with secret enemies. Many

twelfth house people share with me they feel they are betrayed by friends and lovers whom they trusted. Sometimes twelfth house people experience jealousy from coworkers, family and friends. Your energy is loving and kind but sometimes people might want what you have for themselves. When you have good blessings in your life, many people may feel upset if they are struggling. Many clients with twelfth house planets have always asked me about secret enemies, and my theory on this phenomenon is that it's associated with the twelfth house.

From my own experience as a twelfth house person, I have felt that I had secret enemies in my life. My own experience involved people at work or in my career. As twelfth house people we are very trusting and I find this is what causes us to feel betrayed by those we trusted. The truth is that those we trusted really were not true friends or looking out for our best interests. This is where I believe that our twelfth house illusions cloud our perception of others. Of course when we feel hurt or betrayed, we call it secret enemies because these were people that we were loyal to and trusted.

I find that twelfth house people do have people in their lives that do not have the best intentions, but everyone can experience this. I think it is more painful for you because you are trusting and see the good in people. When people let you down, it can feel like a secret enemy. The problem is how you see people because you often see people with rose-colored glasses and believe they have a similar heart like you. The truth is that many people do not trust and love as unconditionally as you do. Do not let "secret enemies" change who you are. Do not allow the pain that others cause you when they let you down to change your good heart. Continue to be who you are and understand that people are human and have weaknesses. Try to forgive those who you feel abandoned and betrayed you in secret. When you feel blindsided and hurt, it is natural to see the people who hurt you as a secret enemy. You never saw it coming and never believed they would hurt you so it is natural that it takes more time to heal from these experiences.

Chapter Ten

Sun, Moon, Venus & North Node: A Deeper Look

Sun in the Twelfth House

Having the Sun in the twelfth house is a special placement. The twelfth house is ruled by Pisces. Everything that is spiritual and mystical represents the energy of this placement. You are very sensitive to others and feel people's pain. You are someone who wears your heart on your sleeve and you are very compassionate. The Sun represents your main identity, and when the Sun is here it makes your personality very secret and hidden. Other people perceive you as mysterious and shy. Most people have no idea how deep, spiritual, caring and sensitive you are.

When the Sun is in the twelfth house, you will have many unexplained experiences and psychic abilities. I have researched the twelfth house for many years and have always been fascinated by it. I noticed that most people that have Sun in the twelfth house were spiritual and interested in astrology, psychology and new age topics. Many times when I did a chart for someone that was a social worker, psychologist, energy healer or astrologer they had the Sun in the twelfth house.

Another similarity I found with people who had the Sun in the twelfth house was father figure issues. Almost every time I did the chart for someone with this placement, they would share with me stories about their absent or missing father figure. Some shared with me that their father had passed away when they were young, parents divorced or separated or that they never had a relationship with their father because they were distant. Some shared with me that they never had even known their father. I have heard many shocking stories about the father figure. After years of research, I found that 95% of the time someone with the Sun in the twelfth house would share with me that their father suffered from some type of addiction, often with alcohol. I started wondering if this was due to the Neptune energy that rules the sign Pisces that rules this house. Neptune rules alcohol, drugs and spirituality.

If your Sun is in the twelfth house, you might not have realized that your father struggled with certain issues until you got older and moved out of the house. You might feel like you do not have a connection or bond with your father figure even if he was around. An absent or missing father figure could be physically, emotionally and mentally. Absent means they are not involved in your life, activities and might not live in the home. There is a lack of closeness with the father when the Sun is placed here. This does not mean that it will stay this way forever. I know a lot of twelfth house Sun people that share with me that as they get older the relationship grows stronger with their father. The good news is that when you grow up this relationship can change and become more positive with effort. When you are young and growing up there was a mystery about your father. There were secrets.

A lot of times your father figure may have suffered from depression or anxiety and this caused him to withdraw from you and the family. Maybe he worked a lot and was never home. Being a workaholic might have been your father's addiction, and when he would come home he was so tired he would just sleep. He might not have come to your school events or games because of working all the time. I find this energy manifests in many ways. Even if there are no addiction issues that the father struggles with, you might not feel you have a father even when you do. I think that this karmic learning happens to help twelfth house Sun people seek a connection with their true father, which is the Creator, God and Universe.

When the Sun is in the twelfth house, it is your destiny to serve others. This is the house of service. When you have this placement you will enjoy helping other people and may find that you have to put other people's needs and wants before your own. You often do that naturally because you are compassionate and selfless. You are truly very self-sacrificing by nature. You often ignore yourself and your own needs.

The energy of the twelfth house is about giving and you do that naturally. You enjoy taking care of your friends and family while forgetting yourself in the midst of your helping. You are destined to do that. You are meant to help others, but just remember that you need to have a good balance in your life. You need to learn to develop boundaries between yourself and other people. You need to learn to take care of yourself too. It is hard to pour from an empty cup. You need to fill yourself up first and then you will be better equipped to help others in a deeper way.

You are intuitive and empathic. Your energy is wide open. When you were younger and growing up, you felt everything. You absorbed other people's emotions. You might not have even realized how much your own mood was affected by being around people in general. If other people were sad, then you would feel sad. If they were happy you would feel happy. You often felt like you did not know where you began or someone else ended, because you felt their pain. You often felt like there was a sign on your back that read, "Come to me for healing. Come to me for help. Come to me if you want to learn about spirituality and cosmic consciousness." You have a sign on your back that people are very drawn to you like moths to a flame. It is a different energy from the eighth house. The twelfth house is a more compassionate, mystical, spiritual and artistic energy.

The twelfth house Sun will make you mystical, spiritual, enlightened and advanced, and you will have a higher energy, a higher level of consciousness. The reason is because this house rules cosmic consciousness. Connecting with the divine will come easy for you. You will realize from a young age that you are not just a physical body, you are a soul. The eighth and twelfth houses are both special houses. The twelfth house is more advanced spiritually and it is a lighter energy than the eighth house. Having the Sun in the twelfth house can bring troubles and secret enemies. Anything secret and hidden lives here, and when your main identity is placed in this house you will find that you have a secretive nature and may attract others who are secretive.

You might not even realize your true identity, and there might be a lot about yourself you don't even know. Other people might think they know you, but you often keep your interests and thoughts private. You are good at hiding your true emotions. You can appear shy, quiet and observant. The sign the Sun is in can change the expression of your energy. For example, if your Sun is in Aries, you are going to be more bold, assertive and vocal. If the Sun is in Leo, you might want to be in the limelight more than most twelfth house people, although the Leo energy will be toned down quite a bit by twelfth house placement. Sometimes twelfth house Sun people are forced to be out in the public even though they really do not want to. They are meant to. Many actors, musicians and politicians have twelfth house planets. The Sun in the twelfth is a very good placement for doing any kind of spiritual or artistic work or for working for the government and foreign travel.

Through my research, I have found that many people with Sun in the twelfth house are attracted to the military or being a part of an organization where everyone dresses alike, behaves alike and acts alike. Joining the military, a Buddhist convent, becoming a nun, priest or rabbi are all related to this placement. Being hidden away, escaping from the world in some way or having a structure where everyone is out for a common mission and goal is a common pursuit. You like your alone time and need it to recover from social situations especially if you work outside the home.

You might seem very social to others but you are an introvert at heart. Everyone might think that you are an extrovert because you can be talkative and friendly and you like to be around a few people to an extent, but you have to have time alone and like to balance both. Some twelfth house Sun people do not like being around people at all and avoid large groups of people. You probably will not enjoy being in large crowds, because you feel overwhelmed by the energy. Small groups or hanging out with one or two friends would benefit you.

Many Sun in the twelfth house people share with me that they have experiences where they detach from their bodies and some actually leave their body through astral projection. You might feel like you are outside your body looking in on yourself, like it is a dream. It is a strange feeling and hard to explain. I have had it happen to me, especially when I was younger. Now that I am older, it is something that rarely happens anymore. You might feel like you are floating around and that you are not inside your body. It is important for you to do grounding exercises and to feel the earth beneath your feet. When you are in large crowds you might experience this more often. You might feel like you are detached from your body and question your reality. This is a physical and emotional experience that many twelfth house people have at some time in their lives.

A beneficial technique that can help is to balance your energy through grounding exercises and breathing techniques. This is another reason it is important for Sun in the twelfth house people to avoid drugs and alcohol. You have a natural ability to absorb everything in your environment and connect spiritually with higher levels of consciousness, so mind-altering substances can really have a negative impact on your mood, mind, health and physical body. This is something to be mindful of.

The twelfth house is associated with addiction. I believe it is the desire to escape from the world that can lead you to experimenting with drugs and alcohol at some time in your life. Alcohol is often used to numb the emotions and to sleep. As a twelfth house person, you will be very sensitive and feel everyone's suffering so you need a break and a way to escape in a healthy way. You just need to be careful about using alcohol and other addictive behaviors to escape from reality. Controlling other addictive behaviors like eating, working, exercising and anything that becomes excessive and a way to escape your problems is a lesson of the twelfth house.

You care a lot and sometimes other people do not realize how deeply they hurt you. You can feel hurt by the words of others and their selfish actions. You will often hide, repress and keep your hurt feelings secret. Sometimes it is because you are not sure how to express it in words, and other times it is because you want to keep peaceful relationships. You do not feel comfortable with anger or confrontation. You can stuff your negative emotions inside, and when this happens you eventually blow up. You can show anger unexpectedly, and other people are often shocked because they don't see you angry very often. It will depend on what sign your Moon is in as well. For instance, I have the Moon in Aries and it takes a lot to make me express my frustration and it is usually impulsive. The good news is that I get over it quickly and move on. The lesson for Sun in the twelfth house people is that you need to try to take time for self-care and to balance your own energy.

It is important for you to have a spiritual path. Since this is the house of service or suffering, you will need to put your spiritual path first. You can find your own unique belief system and religion to follow, it does not matter which one as long as you have a way to go within to seek spiritual knowledge. When the Sun is in the twelfth house you will have a strong desire to seek spiritual knowledge. With your main identity placed here you are born with an interest in astrology, healing, numerology, meditation, yoga and any alternative practice. Since part of your spiritual journey is helping others, you are drawn to nursing, medicine, social work, counseling, working with children. Any career where you can express your artistic and creative abilities such as music, painting or acting. One famous twelfth house person was Johnny Cash. He had his Sun in Pisces in the twelfth house and he was a gifted musician. He struggled with addiction for most of his life because he was trying to escape the pain of losing his younger brother from a tragic accident when he was young. Another famous twelfth house Sun actress is Meryl Streep. She is known for her amazing acting ability and to be able to play deeply emotional characters. There are even a few Presidents who are twelfth house Suns like Bill Clinton and Joe Biden.

Twelfth house Sun blesses you with faith and hope. This can help you find your way out of depression, pull yourself up out of the hurt of heartbreak, and move forward in the world after loss. You will be able to see the spiritual reasons that things happen and try to find the silver lining. You benefit by serving others and helping them heal from similar wounds. Your empathy is extraordinary and you are capable of truly putting yourself in other people's shoes and bringing them comfort. You are blessed with many spiritual gifts such as psychic abilities, mystical experiences, connection to others, intuition, and the ability to help others. Many twelfth house Sun people tell me that they always feel alone. It seems loneliness is a part of the twelfth house person's mission. Feeling alone forces you to seek the meaning of life which is a blessing in disguise. All of these blessings help you overcome many obstacles that you might face. You are destined to seek answers to life's complex problems such as, "Why am I here, what is the purpose of this, why do people suffer?" You are destined to find all these answers and are capable of sharing your wisdom with others.

Moon in the Twelfth House

When the Moon is placed in the twelfth house you will have

a deep emotional nature. The Moon represents our instincts, urges, natural feelings and emotions. You will often hide these feelings and have difficulty expressing them. When the Moon is in the twelfth house your emotional nature is kept very secret and hidden from others due to the natural tendency you have to withdraw and hide your true nature. The Moon placed here will make you extremely sensitive. Many people with twelfth house planets have shared with me that they feel so deeply and are wide open to the environment. You try to hide your true feelings because you are very emotional, compassionate and sensitive to others and your environment.

You have a natural tendency to want to take care of others and attract people that have problems. You attract people with pain who need healing. You are aware that you want to help other people from a young age. Many people with the Moon in the twelfth house share with me that they feel drained emotionally, physically and energy wise by being around too many people. You might experience more intense empathic abilities more than any other planet in the twelfth. The Moon placed here is powerful, and you are affected greatly by the cycles of the Moon. You react intuitively and deeply to things, and benefit by processing your emotions.

When the Moon is placed in the twelfth house you might fear being vulnerable due to your sensitive nature. You might sometimes feel like you don't know your own emotions and you are really good at hiding what you feel. After researching the Moon in the twelfth house for several years, I have found a few common shared experiences from clients. First, the Moon represents the mother figure in your life. Often when the Moon is in the twelfth house, the mother figure has some type of emotional need. Sometimes you might feel like you are more of a parent to your mother. There is a role reversal experience that sometimes happens with this placement. Many twelfth house moon people tell me they feel responsible for the mother figure's well-being, mental health and stability. You might feel like you have a karmic debt to pay to your mother.

Sometimes your mother might fight with depression or anxiety and might be dependent on others, or you felt as a child that you have to be strong and take care of her. You might take on the role of caretaker to your mother from a young age. You may feel like an older sister or even a parent to your mother at times. Many twelfth house Moon people share with me that they felt too responsible at a young age. They have shared with me that they feel they had to grow up way too quickly and did not get the adequate nurturing they needed. The positive side of this placement is that sometimes there is another strong female in your life, like a grandmother who serves in the role of mother to you. You might also find a female role model that you connect with that mentors you throughout your life.

The second thing that many clients share with me that have this placement is that there is a strong bond with the mother. Even if there were problems with your mother you will feel deeply connected to her. Even when there is pain, heartache or heavy responsibilities surrounding the relationship with your mother you will feel intense loyalty towards your mother. The third thing I see with this placement is that there is some type of spiritual gift that you inherit from your mother or the maternal side of the family. You may inherit the gift of intuition, deep dreams, faith and clairvoyance. When the Moon is placed in the twelfth house, you will learn a lot about spirituality from your mother. Your mother may be a very prominent figure in your life who shapes your spiritual path, which is a blessing.

When the Moon is placed in the twelfth house you will be very artistic, creative and possibly have writing talents because you like to express your deep emotions. You like to serve others and help those who suffer and are even more vulnerable and sensitive to other people's energies. You need to learn to build boundaries around yourself to protect your energy field. Meditation can be a great source of comfort for people with Moon in the twelfth house. Journaling your feelings and listening to music can soothe you and help you heal. You may have musical abilities and artistic talents that you can use to help others.

You might feel isolated and different from other people in your life. Sometimes you have a hard time knowing what you truly feel. The Moon placed in the twelfth house will hide some of your inclinations, tendencies and urges causing you to feel unable to express certain emotions. You might feel there is a fog around your ability to communicate what you feel. You can sometimes doubt your own emotional reactions and keep them secret from others due to shyness. A common twelfth house theme is experiencing difficulties expressing the energy of the planet that falls here. You might feel things very deeply but find difficulty speaking the words to describe these feelings.

This placement reminds me of a person I dated back in my college days. He was very smart and intelligent but he was unable to express himself or his emotions in a clear way. He was a very deep person and had a lot of planets in the eighth house. His Moon was in the twelfth house and I remember he wanted to tell me something one night. We stood outside for over 30 minutes in dead silence and he could not express it. He could not express what he felt and after 30 minutes he said he loved me. It took him that long to tell me as he was painfully shy. It hurt me to watch him struggle to express in words what he wanted to tell me.

The Moon in the twelfth will bless you with a deep, emotional nature. You will feel mystical and naturally spiritual. You will feel like words just do not do justice to how you truly feel inside. You will need an outlet for your creative and artistic abilities. Having the Moon placed here is a beautiful placement, blessing you with compassion and kindness.

Venus in the Twelfth House

When Venus is placed in the twelfth house you will have a very secretive love nature. The planet Venus rules your love nature and relationships. Venus will show how to express your love and creativity. You will have a very mystical belief in love. You will keep your feelings hidden and they are very deep. Other people might perceive you as secretive and mysterious. A positive thing about having Venus placed in the twelfth house is that it blesses you with artistic abilities. You will have an ability to write poetry, music, plays, and novels. You have many creative talents even if you do not fully trust your abilities. You will appear illusive to other people and they will see you as beautiful and maybe even unattainable. If Venus is placed in the twelfth house, I recommend that you put a statue of a beautiful goddess facing the doorway when people come into your home. You possess a certain beauty that people are drawn to and you give off a very feminine vibe. You can appear fragile to others and attract people who do not feel good about themselves. They are drawn to you for your gifts. This will help protect against people that want to possess you and win you over for their own selfish motives. You attract the opposite sex and there is something about you they want to own and win over, but they often leave once they take it from you. You have to be cautious who you trust with your heart, soul and body.

You will have a deep love for spirituality and an innate sense of intuition that helps you look within. The struggle of having Venus placed in the twelfth house is your inability to truly express your feelings of love in an easy way. It might be more difficult for you to share how you feel with those you love and you might find it easier to write it in poetry, or keep it secret and love them from afar. The sign that Venus is in will also affect you in positive and negative ways. For instance, if Venus is in Virgo you will be very shy and afraid of being hurt. It might take a special person to pull you out of that shyness.

For the most part, you will hide your deep feelings and love nature from yourself and others. Hiding things can manifest as self-denial, self-illusion, delusions, and be things that you do not see clearly. Neptune rules Pisces, the ruler of the twelfth house. Neptune is the culprit that creates illusions and a fog around how you perceive your feelings and how you express your affection for others.

From my research, many twelfth house Venus people have shared with me stories of heartbreak and unhealthy relationships. At some time in your life you may experience secret love and a secret love affair. Now this secret love might not be acted upon or expressed, but it will most likely affect you at some time in your life. You might be in love with someone and never tell them, keeping your true feelings hidden. Many astrology books relate the twelfth house Venus with clandestine love affairs, which just means secret or hidden from others. You might experience situations where you fall in love with someone who is not free such as loving someone you can't be with because they are married, a coworker, your supervisor, someone much younger or older than you or someone inappropriate in society's eyes. You can experience a barrier that prevents you from expressing your true feelings for someone.

Due to this energy, you might experience heartache and loss through seeking a soul mate. Another way this energy manifests is that you might act on your secret love and share intimacy with them and have a deep bond that you keep secret from everyone. Sometimes only you and your lover are aware of the relationship. The pain of this placement comes through loss of love, and when things are secret there are often difficulties in having what you truly want. The twelfth house is associated with sacrifice. You might feel you have to sacrifice your love due to many factors. You have to give up someone that you love, or you feel that they abandon you creating a wound. It might be difficult for you to trust people again after these hidden affairs. You may develop fears of falling in love or being in relationships.

Many clients with Venus in the twelfth house have shared stories with me concerning love and relationships. A common theme is that you feel that you love someone who is not free and you can't be with them publicly. The karma of this placement makes a destiny with your true love hard to attain. Sometimes your secret feelings are never acted upon and you won't have affairs. Although you will experience secret feelings that you hide deep inside, and often keep these feelings behind the scenes and never tell anyone. You might feel that these types of relationships continue throughout your life and that you find yourself in unhappy relationships or marriages.

When Venus is placed in the twelfth house, you need a spiritual partner or someone who accepts this part of you and cherishes your journey. If you do not find someone that is on your spiritual level (mentally, emotionally and physically) then you will feel restless and be seeking something. The thing you are seeking is your own soul, but you often feel that it is a soul mate that you are seeking. You believe in destiny and that there is a special person chosen for you out in the world. This belief and illusion can lead to painful emotional wounds.

The emotional wounds you experience come from your extremely romanticized view of love. You are very affectionate when you love someone and you often only see the positive side of someone's personality. You have the Neptune glasses on that cloud your vision and you often put people on a pedestal when you love them. You also are withdrawn and wait for someone to share their love for you first. You do not make the first move due to your deep feelings and fears that the other person might not reciprocate. The sign that Venus is placed in will also transform the energy. For instance, if you have Venus in Aries in the twelfth, you may be more vocal and expressive than someone with Venus in Pisces. For the most part though, you are going to hide unless you know that someone feels the same way first. You struggle due to fears that someone will not feel the same way or they are not as devoted as you are to the relationship. This reality can cause deep hurt and loneliness for you. You are constantly searching for someone that can fulfill your spiritual desires and needs. I find many twelfth house Venus clients have had many heartbreaks and felt let down in love. They have put a wall up around themselves and are afraid to trust so they block themselves from attracting a healthy loving relationship.

You know what pain in love feels like. You are truly a wounded healer as far as relationship karma goes. You are the kind of person that understands relationship issues, divorce and breakups. You are able to feel other people's pain easily and you understand how love can be beautiful and also painful. The positive thing about Venus in the twelfth house is that you are a very passionate, compassionate, kind, loyal person when someone wins your heart. If you fall in love with someone you will give them your heart and the shirt off your back. This placement blesses you with the ability to love unconditionally.

North Node in Pisces or the Twelfth House

The North Node in your chart represents your soul mission this lifetime. At the age of 27 through 30 you will experience your first Saturn Return. During this time you will start feeling the pull towards your North Node for the very first time. Prior to this age, you are living in the past connected to your South Node. The South Node is your past life mission and what your soul has already mastered. The planet Saturn returns to where it was in your birth chart every 27 to 30 years stirring up karmic lessons and learning to ensure that you master what your soul came here to accomplish. The Saturn Return can be a painful time in your life where you are forced to change and be reborn into a new person. It is important to study which house and sign in which the North Node is placed in your natal chart.

The North Node in Pisces or twelfth house is my favorite node. One of the reasons is that there are a lot of people in my life that I care about that have these nodes. Virgo is the opposite sign of Pisces and is known as the servant and worker of the zodiac. Virgos tend to worry and over-analyze things. Virgo is service-oriented and enjoys helping others in a practical way. They are analytical and extremely organized. In past lifetimes, the Virgo South Node person has mastered the eye for detail and focusing on reality. If North Node is in Pisces you have mastered being a Virgo. You are naturally smart and intelligent, and love learning things. You also have an eye for seeing things that need fixing. You also probably have a gift for writing and teaching. At heart, you are conscientious and shy. Virgo is also known as the perfectionist of the zodiac.

When the South Node is placed in Virgo you are learning to move away from Virgo traits that no longer serve you. The negative personality traits of Virgo need to be let go of and you are meant to become more like a Pisces. As a North Node Pisces person you are learning to be helpful and help people but in a different way. The way I like to describe it is that you are a person who is learning to become spiritual. You are learning to have trust and faith in a higher power and in the universe by releasing your need to control things. You are learning to let go of your need to have everything organized, planned and perfect. Virgos do not like change and they like to know what is going to happen. You like to be prepared for everything and make lists to organize yourself. You carry these basic Virgo traits within you into this life.

In this lifetime, you are now learning to be a Pisces and to let go of your need for perfection. It can be hard for you because as you move towards your North Node you might feel that you are being lazy if you do not work harder than everyone else. You were a workaholic in past lifetimes and served others selflessly often neglecting your own self-care and life. You might struggle with saying no to others. You can deplete your own energy because of guilt from not doing everything that is asked of you. In this lifetime, Pisces North Node is learning to let go of guilt and burdens. In this lifetime, you are learning to let go of any negative emotions that make you feel trapped and that you have to have things a certain way for you to be perfect, good and worthy of love. You are learning that your own self-worth comes from within and developing a spiritual connection.

You are becoming a Pisces and this means that you must learn to be more compassionate with others and yourself. You are learning to release your anxieties and worries. You are going to feel this pull like a seesaw of going back and forth between feeling worry, obsessing about things and analyzing things. Once you enter your Saturn Return, you will start feeling this pull towards releasing the Virgo traits and becoming more laid-back and relaxed. You will start feeling many things and will feel much more emotional. Clients who have this Node often tell me that they are not emotional people and fight to keep their feelings under control. You might have difficulty expressing your love nature, passionate feelings or sharing your true thoughts with those you care about. As you move into the Pisces energy, you are going to start feeling more raw. Your emotions will start bubbling to the surface.

When you put extra effort into mastering the personality traits of your North Node you will find that changes come easier for you. Resisting the new is what often causes you pain. The more you embrace Pisces energy, the more you will start feeling things. You will become much more emotional than you were in the past. You will cry easily and more often. This might take some time for you to accept and know that this is a new journey. You will experience new parts of you as they emerge. Embrace them, you are learning to be a Pisces. As a Pisces, you are developing compassion and empathy. Pisces people wear their heart on their sleeves, and when you cry, they cry. They feel other people's pain. Pisces are chameleons and absorb the personality, emotions and thoughts of those they are around. Your old Virgo self does not like feeling pain as you intellectualize pain. Virgo doesn't feel the emotional depth of things, but Pisces does.

You are learning to move towards a sense of depth of emotion, becoming more deep and more philosophical. The biggest lesson for a Pisces North Node is to learn not to judge yourself or others so harshly. You have high standards for how you expect others to behave and how you expect to treat others. You were a perfectionist. So you know that no one is perfect all the time. You can do your best to try to be perfect, but you are learning to let go of that need. You need to let go of the South Node Virgo energy. The thing that can help let go of your need to be perfect is to have trust and faith in a higher power. Your mission with this Node is to become spiritual and not to resist it.

The North Node in Pisces or twelfth house is similar to all the energy of the twelfth house. When you have this Node then you have to put spirituality, God and a spiritual path first. You will benefit by studying psychology, astrology, dreams, meditation and yoga. Immersing yourself in twelfth house hobbies and interests will help you move towards mastering this Node. You need to pursue activities that will help you connect with your soul and spirit. You are meant to spend time alone and go within yourself to seek answers.

The way that I describe it is that the old you, the Virgo part of you, wants to be practical and work-focused, completing tasks and achieving goals. You like to be of service doing practical duties such as cooking, cleaning, doing taxes, typing up something for a friend, reading or giving friends advice. Pisces is the opposite of this. Pisces is pulling you to live in the moment and act on what you feel. It might not be practical as emotions often are not something that you are used to expressing. The

Neptune energy causes a little bit of illusion and mystical views of things. This new energy shift can be scary to a Virgo South Node because it's new and different. The North Node is always new territory. You are opening up and learning to feel free and comfortable expressing your true nature and what you really think and feel. You need to share parts of yourself that you have never shared before, because the old you is very shy and very cautious about being vulnerable. It is not that you do not trust people, it is that you are conscientious and fear rejection.

Becoming a Pisces is stepping out there on a cliff and trusting if you step off that somebody will catch you and there is a higher power that is there for you that will lift you up and make sure that you are protected. North Node in Pisces will make you a healer and a person who understands what others are going through because you feel it. This Node wants you to serve in an emotional, spiritual type of way, and not in the practical basic hands-on way like your old Virgo self. Pisces need to feel very connected to people. You love music, and listening to music is healing and relaxes you. Having healthy relationships is crucial for you. Being able to trust someone and be intimate is a big deal for you. You are used to being reserved. You are learning to share your body, mind, heart and soul with another human being. You do not readily do that as you are very picky about who you choose to love and allow to get close to you. In this lifetime, the Pisces North Node is pushing you to trust and have faith. You are meant to be intimate and vulnerable with others this lifetime.

You are learning to accept people's flaws without judging them. You need to accept that it is okay if things are not always organized, planned and controlled, or work out the exact way you want them to. You are meant to focus instead on believing things are meant to be for a reason. You are learning to develop a connection with God. Balancing your mind, body and spirit will help you heal. Pisces North Node has to have time alone. As you get older, you will feel that you need to withdraw and have time to be alone. You might feel lazy spending time alone not working or doing tasks. You are meant to become more peaceful and simple. Doing less is your mantra. In your past lives you were used to doing, serving, doing, serving and repeat. You must turn your focus on going within and caring for yourself.

You need to have a good balance and you also have to work to support yourself, but it is not going to be the focus. The focus is going to change for you because when you work you will need it to be meaningful. It can't be dutiful work like a Virgo. It must be meaningful to you or you will not be fulfilled. You need to find a job that is meaningful to you or you can feel depressed and isolated. People in your life need to realize that as you get older you are going to become more reclusive and withdrawn from the physical world. It does not mean that you will be withdrawn emotionally from your loved ones, but you will need time alone this lifetime to balance your energies. You are meant to let go and surrender to the moment and to your soul mission this lifetime which is learning to be a spiritual person.

Chapter Eleven

Finding a Spiritual Path

One of the most important lessons that twelfth house people must learn is how to be spiritual and find a spiritual path. There is a difference between being spiritual versus being religious. You are learning that all religious paths lead to God and that there is not just one right path. It might take you some time to find the right path for you. You must find a spiritual path because you are a special soul; it is your destiny. You are born feeling different and have natural healing abilities. You understand other people's pain because you have felt the same pain. You are able to put yourself in other people's shoes and you truly empathize with the pain others feel. This is what makes you a natural therapist and counselor. Twelfth house people are drawn to careers where they can help other people discuss their pain. Helping others heal also helps you heal.

The twelfth house rules the subconscious and everything that is deep and spiritual in our world. As a twelfth house person, you are able to connect to different realms and energies. The subconscious mind is the level of mind that we use when we are connected to our spiritual self. We use the subconscious mind when we dream, meditate, practice relaxation and use our imagination. As a twelfth house person, you will have a lot of mystical experiences because your subconscious abilities are heightened. You can dream deeper than most people and your dreams are vivid. Utilizing your dreams and analyzing the symbols is a routine that can benefit you as you often dream of things that are coming in the future. Listening to your subconscious thoughts, emotions and ideas will help you on your spiritual journey.

No matter how hard life becomes or how much twelfth house

people go through, they always have a belief in something greater than themselves. I have yet to meet a twelfth house person that does not have some type of spiritual belief system that brings them comfort and strength in times of need. You will benefit through studying different spiritual techniques and new age philosophies. The goal is for you to learn how to apply these spiritual practices into your life. Many twelfth house people benefit from meditation and contemplation. Spending time in nature can also bring you peace and a deeper connection to God. You are always seeking to connect to your spirit and soul. Anything you can do to connect and ground yourself will help you grow stronger and develop a spiritual outlook that will help you throughout your life.

Twelfth house people enjoy helping other people and this is also part of your spiritual journey. You are meant to find some type of outlet for your spiritual gifts and assisting others in life lessons can bring you closer to the divine. Through selfless service, twelfth house people often feel a sense of purpose and a deeper connection with the universe. You realize that you are one with everyone and everything in this world. You are not separate and that is why you feel everyone's pain. Your energy is wide open and taps into the energies of others easily.

I remember being young and I always had a spiritual belief and a fascination with angels, but I was not raised to be religious. I always had a vivid imagination and was a deep dreamer. I remember buying dream books and looking up the symbols and analyzing them. Everyone who knew me always would hear about my dreams and I would always listen to my dreams and heed their warnings. I came to believe this was God's way of protecting me and preparing me for the future. I started researching this and discussing dreams with other twelfth house people, and they too shared similar stories. Almost all twelfth house people love to sleep and dream. I did a survey in my twelfth house astrology group and asked members about their dreams. It was no surprise that many shared dreaming about the future and how dreams have changed their lives. Dreaming occurs in the subconscious levels of the mind and connects us to our soul. Carl Jung said an "unexamined dream is like an unopened letter" and includes important spiritual messages. In the Bible, dreams are mentioned many times and God gave his people dreams at night to help guide them on their spiritual path.

I think the key to finding a spiritual path is to be open-minded. I have met people with planets in the twelfth house that are Christian, Buddhist, Hindu, Wiccan and Jewish. Some twelfth house people do not like to label their spiritual beliefs and do not associate with going to church and being part of a group. Some tell me they would rather be alone in their house meditating and journaling on Sundays. The important thing to remember is there is no right or wrong path. The important thing is that you find something that helps you connect to your soul purpose and the reason you are here on earth.

Chapter Twelve

Planets in the Twelfth House

Sun in the Twelfth

I have Sun in the 12th house. I never met my father due to him being an alcoholic and inflicting abuse on my mother. I found my connection to God and realized he is my true parent.
– R.L., Louisiana

When the sun is placed in the twelfth house, you are a person who enjoys alone time. You like to escape from the world and seclude yourself from the realities of life. You enjoy your quiet time and need a peaceful environment in order to survive. You are extremely sensitive and have a very spiritual nature. You are born intuitive and with an inner belief about a higher power. You are drawn to things that are hidden and mystical. You attract people that have problems and are always seeking to help those who are suffering. You are blessed with psychic abilities and have empathic sensitivity that you can utilize to help others in a deeper way. You feel other people's pain and try hard to help others feel better. You attract the downtrodden and outcasts of society. You prefer to work behind the scenes in seclusion and are a private person. Your emotions are strong and can lead to depression and anxiety. You seem to struggle in groups and find yourself feeling different from others. You feel uncomfortable in large groups and prefer small group or one on one interaction.

You have a desire to escape from the world and can find yourself on a good path or bad path. The good path for you is when you decide that you will pursue spirituality, meditation and service to others, and the bad path for you is when you turn to drugs such as alcohol. You are very susceptible to addiction and need to be cautious about using any types of substances that alter your mind or body. You can use these things as a crutch to numb yourself from the pain you feel. You are a person who must learn to become spiritual and to serve others less fortunate. Your life will be much easier if you learn how to protect yourself and to find balance between your emotional and practical sides.

You have father figure issues. Your father probably was not a strong presence in your life and might have died when you were younger. If he was in your life, you always felt that he was emotionally unavailable to you. You tried hard to overcome your pain and seek to find a father figure in those that you meet. You can attract relationship partners that are not healthy for you and that play out your trauma bond with your own father. You want others to love you and sometimes see people for how you want them to be, not as they really are. Your idealistic nature can get you hurt and cause you great pain. You must learn to put God first in your life and seek a greater spiritual connection to the universe to overcome your deep loneliness and feelings of not having a true family. You are truly blessed with extraordinary psychic abilities and can use them to help others.

Moon in the Twelfth

I have Moon in the 12th house and my relationship with my mother was toxic. I had to raise and nurture myself emotionally and mentally. My feelings were always so complicated that I could never figure them out. I feel everything so deeply within and without. It has caused a lot of pain and isolation but also I feel gifted to have this placement due to my intuitive abilities.
– I.M., U.S.A.

When the moon is placed in the twelfth house, you are a person who has a very spiritual emotional nature. Your intuition and ability to read other people's emotions is truly a gift. Your emotional nature is often kept secret and hidden from others. Still waters run deep with you and you often hide your true intense emotions from others. You are a person who must have time to withdraw on your own and spend time away from the hustle and bustle of the world. You benefit by listening to soothing music and having beautiful art surrounding you. Music is very important to you and brings you comfort in times of stress. You might have artistic talents that you keep hidden because you are afraid that you are not "good enough" to perform them. You are hard on yourself and would benefit from learning how to express your intricate emotions through writing, journaling and recording dreams. Your emotional nature is sensitive, and you will suffer from emotional ups and downs in your life. The natural process of emotions is very fascinating to you and you may feel depressed often. You do not necessarily need medication to treat these subdued feelings but would benefit by talking about them, writing about them, or accepting them as a part of you. Sometimes you do not know if it is your pain or that of others that you are feeling.

You feel other people's thoughts, emotions and suffering, and absorb that within yourself. You like to run away and hide, but you have much to give the world. Your spiritual gifts are magnificent, and you genuinely care about helping people. You often find yourself drawn into the helping professions caring for the sick, elderly, disabled or with children. Just make sure you take enough time for yourself, and your own inner growth and healing.

The relationship you had with your mother was complex. You might have felt as if you were the "parent" and your mother was the child. You were dependable and felt responsible for your mother figure and her happiness. You may have experienced your mother figure as emotionally vulnerable, weak or unstable, and as someone who "needed you to be strong". Your mother may have suffered from depression, sadness or mental illness. She may have also been spiritual and blessed you with many of her spiritual teachings. This type of parental relationship caused an emotional wound. If you had to take care of your mother, you might have not had your own emotional needs met. You felt that you could always do that on your own, making it hard for you to open up emotionally to others.

You may fear being vulnerable because you know what can happen and you don't want to become like your mother. Even though you have mother figure issues, you often have an unspeakable bond with your mother and are extremely loyal to her regardless of the situation you had as a child. You benefit from your mother and may inherit her spiritual gifts or abilities, and she might have been a strong spiritual role model in your life by teaching you what is really important versus what is superficial.

Venus in the Twelfth

I always feel like I will never be able to find love with this placement. I find I attract men who are liars, cheaters, are taken and con artists. I have to set boundaries.
– M.C., U.S.A.

When Venus is placed in the twelfth house, you are a person who hides your romantic feelings and relationships. The twelfth house is known as the "House of Suffering". The energy that rules this house is kept hidden or secret. The deep secrets about your own personality as well as your emotions are locked within you. This placement is an indicator of suffering through love affairs and heartache at some time in your life. The positive energy of this placement is that you are also protected by what seems like a guardian angel watching over you. When you are at your lowest point and almost ready to give up hope, the universe answers your prayers in many ways. You are always protected, and you are guarded more than others around you by invisible forces.

You are destined to experience clandestine or secret love affairs. This happens because your expression of love is kept secret from others. Your initial emotion of love is held within and sometimes never expressed. You might often find yourself in love with someone that is not free. You may fall in love with someone who is already married or committed to someone else. I have studied several charts with this placement, and almost every time, the client reveals to me that they either had an affair, were in love with someone they could not be with, or they were in love with someone and never let them know.

You will experience hidden feelings or secret love affairs at some time in your life. Sometimes the feelings are acted on and other times you will keep them hidden and repressed. You may not cheat on your partner, but you will have "emotional affairs" because of the energy of this placement. Even the most moral, committed and happily married individual can fall prey to this placement. This can be extremely difficult for you, but with understanding and compassion you will eventually heal. You can suffer as a result of the relationships that you find yourself in. It is important for you to truly look within and be honest about your emotions. You have a tendency to be attracted to partners that have some type of pain in their life. You are attracted to partners who have been wounded. You fall in love with people that need your help and you feel you need to take care of in some way.

You can attract unhealthy partners that might not be mentally stable, and this can manifest as depression. You are spiritual and can fall in love easily with partners that are spiritual. Love and spirituality go hand and hand for you. Just be cautious when you have feelings for others. Sometimes you can put people up on a pedestal and have illusions about how someone truly is because you only see the good in others. You can be blinded by love and ignore all the red flags of disaster before it is too late. You will naturally love others who are wounded, outcasts or those that people make fun of. You have great compassion for those who suffer and are different. Sometimes you can get involved in relationships with partners that have addiction issues such as alcoholism. You are a natural codependent when you are in relationships and need to be careful not to neglect yourself for others. You have to learn to first love yourself before you can truly love others in a healthy way.

You will experience relationships like the ones described above but remember that it is not your fault. The energy of this placement might eventually lead you into situations similar to the ones above. You are destined to experience secretive relationships and secret love affairs at some time in your life. You can learn about this energy and choose to approach it in a different way. Being aware of this energy can help you prevent certain situations and relationships from developing.

Mars in the Twelfth

I am unable to express my anger and I repress it inside. I can get sick from not allowing myself to show my anger but it is something that illudes me. I am not even sure how to express it. I find that music helps me cope with my intense feelings and I have a strong drive to learn about God and find a spiritual path.
– E.F., California

When Mars is placed in the twelfth house, you are a person who hides your true feelings and desires. You have a strong spiritual nature and are very intuitive. You are driven and like to delve into the depths of your own mind and the minds of others. Your selfish desires are often hidden from others and no one really knows what you really want. Sometimes your desires and actions are influenced by a force outside yourself. You often feel an overwhelming sense of mission, but avoid opening up to others because of your own unconscious fears.

You may feel repressed and have an inability to express your restless nature outwardly. You tend to internalize your passions and intense feelings, finding them difficult to express. You will feel angry like most people, but it will be difficult for you to express it. You often turn your anger onto yourself, which can cause health problems. You should try to meditate every day to help relieve your pent-up energy. You have a strong desire to serve others and help those that are wounded. You can fight for those that are abused, abandoned and alone. You enjoy rescuing people and like to feel that you are appreciated for your kind actions. You can fluctuate between extremes of anger and then show extreme compassion. Your compassionate nature is intensified with this placement and sometimes you might neglect yourself for others. You will benefit by trying to understand your complex nature by utilizing writing, journaling and spiritual pursuits.

There is a danger for you to become involved with alcohol or other self-destructive behaviors. You need to face your problems head-on and not blame yourself for everything that happens. You may try to escape from your painful experiences and find it hard to face daily life. You are prone to depression, which often is a natural part of your personality. You can overcome your loneliness by seeking things that have meaning and finding your own sense of spirituality. You may need to talk to a counselor about your problems and emotions, which will create a healthy outlet for your pent-up feelings. You like to hide your problems from others and put a lot of effort and energy into being secretive about your faults. You need to be careful and watch out when you are driving or operating machinery. You are vulnerable to cuts and injuries, and may have to have surgery at some time in your life.

Your relationship with your father is something that causes you pain. In childhood, your father might have suffered with alcoholism and was not emotionally or physically there for you. You may have argued with your father and might have felt like you had to take care of him because of his weaknesses.

You feel like you have an absent or missing father figure and are always seeking something from others, which is acceptance. When you turn your energy towards spirituality and connecting with your higher power you will feel more secure. Be careful not to allow your father's problems to become your own. You need to be cautious about using alcohol or drugs because you are highly susceptible to addiction.

The blessing of this placement is a gift of intense spirituality and compassion. You need to learn to love yourself and open yourself up to others. You will benefit by learning to express yourself freely and to trust that others will appreciate your honesty. You will always feel that anger is a difficult emotion to deal with, but the more you embrace it, the more you will grow. You will be happier when you stop allowing others to take your power.

Mercury in the Twelfth

My thoughts are deep and just when I want to describe something to someone and express myself it's like I lose the words and become dreamy and scattered.
– L.B., England

When Mercury is placed in the twelfth house, you are a deep thinker and often hide your true thoughts. You are a person who finds it difficult to express yourself to others. You are shy and can find it difficult to let others into your life, because of your private nature. You are a deep thinker and have a very perceptive mind. You may not always express yourself and find it difficult to put words to your emotions. Your intuition and first impressions are likely to be accurate. You are bored with practical learning and enjoy imaginative subjects. You enjoy daydreaming and can escape into your mind when you are feeling stress. You need time alone to recover from daily life. It is important that you have the time to be alone with your own thoughts.

You might have psychic experiences and be able to read others' thoughts. You may have flashes of intuition and you would benefit by writing down your insights. You may enjoy writing and find it easier to write down your thoughts than to say them verbally. Writing can be a great healing resource for you. You can feel that your thoughts are deep and you often have difficulty understanding what you think. You can get your thoughts and others' thoughts confused. You are very sensitive to others and the environment that you are in. You can take on the thoughts of others and with practice can control this ability. You have a spiritual mind and enjoy thinking about the meaning of life and spirituality. You can meditate easily and can benefit by quieting your mind and spending time in silence. Your mind reaches great depths, and you are someone who can be hypnotized easily and are highly suggestible.

Jupiter in the Twelfth

I always feel protected like someone is watching over me. Even when I am alone in a room, I feel someone is there helping me like angels are around me.
– T.S., China

When Jupiter is in the twelfth house, you are a person who is born with intuitive gifts. You are shielded from many of the negative energies of the twelfth house. You have a guardian angel that watches over you, that shields you from the pain and suffering often found here. You have a vivid imagination and an optimistic approach to life. You will benefit by doing anything spiritual such as meditation, writing, metaphysics and spirituality. You can connect to spirit easily and are blessed with a deep connection to God. You might seek out this relationship by becoming a nun, priest or rabbi. You love to study ancient knowledge and are attracted to things that are deep and meaningful.

You will have good luck coming to you from spiritual work and service to others. The more you serve others, the more blessings will be given to you. You have a strong desire for alone time and solitude. You enjoy being by yourself and prefer to spend time alone. You are sensitive in large groups and would prefer to spend time thinking, writing and studying deep subjects. Other people in your life will be drawn to you and will enjoy sharing their problems with you. Your outlook on life is upbeat and optimistic. You are able to answer many questions for others on a variety of spiritual topics. You are born with a natural understanding of life and why we are here. You may have grown up in a family that is very different than you and they will not understand your spiritual nature.

You can sacrifice yourself for a greater spiritual cause and are capable of selfless acts of service. You will receive good luck and blessings each time you make a sacrifice for others. The more you give to others, the more you receive. You attract abundance in many areas and are always searching for a deeper connection to the world. You are someone who enjoys spending time in deep thought and you like to try to figure out what is the purpose of life. You do not enjoy superficial subjects and prefer to live a life of asceticism. You realize that true happiness does not come from the outer world of material possessions, but from within and by finding your connection to your spiritual source.

You are blessed with psychic gifts and intuitive abilities.

You can have visions, impressions and dreams that predict the future. You would benefit by keeping a journal next to your bed at night while you sleep. You need to write your dreams down every night, and it will be beneficial to keep a journal so you can start to write down your intuitive impressions throughout the day. You are luckier than most people who have twelfth house planets and you are shielded from the loneliness that usually comes with the twelfth house.

Saturn in the Twelfth

I often feel restricted and unable to express myself well. I am cautious with people and even doubt my own intuition even though it has been right most of my life. I know I need to trust more.
– R.S., Iowa

When Saturn is in the twelfth house, you are a person who tries to repress their fears and doubts. You are a person who may suffer from depression and sadness. You will work very hard to cover up your depression and try to overcome it. You need to be easier on yourself and understand that everyone gets depressed, and sometimes feeling sad is normal. You may suffer from guilty feelings and not truly understand where your guilt comes from. You have a fear of the unknown and of being overwhelmed by your emotions. You are a sensitive person and have escapist tendencies. You like to be alone and have the time to do things in seclusion. Your emotions are strong and you have to work hard to control them. You spend a lot of time controlling your thoughts, emotions and behaviors.

You may suffer from some type of addiction and you are able to repress the urge for the substance with discipline and willpower. You will have problems with relapse if you do not allow yourself to face the emotions and feelings that led to the addiction in the first place. You do not like to be dependent on others and you avoid sharing your painful feelings with them. You will experience pain and feelings of separateness because you will not allow yourself to open up to others or be vulnerable. You are rigid in your behaviors and will use self-control to overcome many unpleasant emotions.

Even though you do not like relying on others to support you, you enjoy others reaching out to you for help. You are often the person that your friends and family turn to for support and understanding. You want to be strong for your family and will set aside your own problems to help them with theirs. Being of service to others will help you break free of your unpleasant guilt and will help you break the chains that you impose upon yourself. You need to embrace your psychic abilities and learn how to use them in a practical way.

Uranus in the Twelfth

I have flashes of insight and visions unexpectedly. Sometimes I just blurt out what I see and feel before thinking. I love to study spiritual topics that are unique and different. I don't like to be forced to believe a certain way or told what I have to do.
– J.B., Missouri

When Uranus is placed in the twelfth house, you are a person who experiences visions of the future. You are gifted with psychic abilities that seem to come to you instantly. You are a person who needs time to be alone. You are reclusive and enjoy studying mystical subjects behind the scenes. You can experience secret love affairs and fall in love with others easily. You often hide your true feelings for those you care about. You enjoy having freedom to study and time alone to expand your mind.

You need to be careful about abusing substances such as alcohol or cigarettes. You can become addicted to substances easily because you like to experience change and find it exciting. You can suffer from your own instability and rebellious nature. You have an addictive type of personality and can find it difficult to give up things that you become obsessed with. Your beliefs about the world are constantly changing. You need to live in an environment that allows you to be free. You have intuitive and psychic abilities that can be used to serve others. You often can see things before they happen and have the gift of clairvoyance.

You need to trust your visions, dreams and perceptions about the future. You would benefit by writing things down and can find that you have a great writing talent. Writing will bring you a sense of peace and will help you balance your restless nature. You need to trust in yourself and allow the universe to send you messages so that you can help uplift others who are suffering. The more you help others who are suffering and allow yourself to change, the more spiritual you will become.

Neptune in the Twelfth

I feel everything. I mean everything. I am so sensitive it's hard to learn boundaries. I was born an artist and can paint and draw naturally.
– R.M., England

When Neptune is placed in the twelfth house, you are a person who suffers from your own compassionate nature. You are extremely sensitive to the emotions in the environment and to other people. You lack protection from the energetic influences that surround you. You easily pick up what others think, feel and believe. You suffer greatly at times because of your sensitivity. You can feel depressed, withdrawn and sad for no reason. You are a loner and prefer to spend time by yourself. You are imaginative and enjoy thinking deeply about life.

You are born psychic and are able to understand things

about people without them telling you. You are like a sponge and absorb everything in the environment. You need to learn how to protect yourself and develop stronger boundaries with others. Others can easily fool you and drain you of your positive energy. You like to believe that everyone is good and spiritual. When you realize that the world can be an evil place, you can become despondent. The realization that people can be mean, evil and abusive disturbs you. You prefer to see everyone as loving, kind and compassionate like you are.

You are interested in life after death and hidden realms. You may repress your true emotions and keep them secret from others. You may feel that others will not understand your spiritual beliefs and nature. The older you get, the more spiritual you will become. You need to be careful not to abuse drugs or alcohol because you are highly sensitive to substances that alter the mind. You are prone to addiction and escaping from your emotional pain. You need to face the pain you feel, and transform it into a spiritual understanding and bond with God. You are blessed with the ability to connect to God through meditation, prayer and journaling. Your life will be happiest when you follow a spiritual path and way of life.

Pluto in the Twelfth

I can be my own worst enemy. I punish myself with my thoughts and get so caught up in negativity and fear that it makes me sullen and depressed at times. I also abuse drugs and alcohol as a way to cope with my confusing emotions.
– E.J., Colorado

When Pluto is in the twelfth house, you are a person who hides your powerful feelings. You like to hide who you really are. You prefer working behind the scenes and like influencing things secretly. You often have a powerful position and give orders

113

to others behind the scenes. No one will ever truly realize the power you have in the world because you like to hide the influence you have. You have a very secretive nature and are always hiding from others. You have intense and passionate emotions that you try to hide, and this can lead to secret love affairs. You can become obsessed with your romantic feelings and find it hard to concentrate. You can become addicted to your own emotions and develop unhealthy relationships with others that are difficult to end.

You are born with psychic abilities and a deep understanding about life. You are naturally spiritual and seek time alone to meditate, write and think about spiritual issues. You can have time where you can deny yourself and give up things for your spiritual path. You have intense sexual desires and may try to become celibate as a test to yourself. You like to push the limits and you enjoy feeling the adrenaline of intense emotional interaction. You are a passionate person, and you enjoy risk-taking behaviors. You need to be careful about getting involved in drugs or alcohol. You can become addicted easily to substances and find it hard to give them up. You bottle up your emotions and keep them secret from others, which can lead to escapism. You feel a powerful need to escape from the world into your imagination or through alcohol. You feel anger intensely and sometimes it turns into a rage that you try to repress and hide. Make sure you learn how to express your powerful emotions in a healthy way, because if not you could become sick.

You will benefit by studying anything spiritual. You need to feel a connection to God, and this is where your wound begins. Your relationship with your father was possibly strained or nonexistent. Your father might have had an addiction to alcohol, a mental illness or may have died at a young age. You must learn how to heal and love yourself. You may feel that you do not have a physical father, and this causes you immense pain and suffering. You will heal your wound when you learn to turn your face towards God, who is your true father. You are destined to seek a spiritual connection with the universe, and this will help you heal your inner wounds.

Chapter Thirteen

Neptune through the Houses

The planet Neptune rules the twelfth house and embodies the mystical and watery energy of Pisces. Neptune energy is funky, unique, calm, mysterious and otherworldly. You will experience the energy of Neptune in your natal chart depending on which house it is placed in your natal chart. You will also be affected by Neptune energy when it is transiting different areas of your life and triggering learning lessons in specific houses.

In your astrology chart, the planet Neptune represents spirituality, enlightenment, illusion and mysticism. The position of Neptune shows where you have a tendency to idolize people and things. You tend to have rose-colored glasses on in the area of life that Neptune influences. Neptune also shows where you suffer emotionally and where you find your connection to spirituality. You have to be careful with Neptune because it can confuse you, deceive you and make you believe something that is not there. Neptune makes you only see the good in people and situations. This can cause you pain and prevent you from seeing things realistically. This planet can bring pain and suffering into your life. The pain Neptune causes can help you become more spiritual in the process. Neptune rules drugs and alcohol, and can show where you might be vulnerable to addiction.

Neptune in the First House

When Neptune is placed in the first house, you are a person who has a dreamy, mystical appearance. Others perceive you as being flighty and it is like you are living in a dream world. You look and act like you are living in another world and your energy is very mysterious. Others may misjudge you and think that you are under the influence of drugs at some time in your life. This may not be true, but the energy you radiate can seem that way. You seem like you are in another dimension or level of awareness, or out of touch with reality. You are extremely sensitive to your environment and you can become vulnerable to negative energy. If people in the environment are positive then you will feel positive, but if they are unhappy, then you will feel unhappy. You absorb and take on the energy that is surrounding you very easily. It is important that you make sure to surround yourself with positive people.

You are a spiritual person and many people recognize your kindness. People feel your compassionate presence immediately and feel your helpful nature. You suffer most from not being able to protect yourself from others' energy, and you need to learn to develop stronger boundaries. You struggle with having to stand up for yourself. You avoid conflict and enjoy escaping from the world. You can live in your imagination and others may feel they can't understand you. You might also feel misunderstood by others. You might feel that you have your head in the clouds and have a hard time being present in the physical realm.

You will benefit by learning to ground yourself and your energy. You need to love and nurture yourself as much as possible. Your greatest challenge is learning to have boundaries and developing the ability to take care of your own needs and not neglect them. You have a tendency to suffer from body image issues, insecurities and may not feel that you are attractive. You need to learn to accept yourself and be less judgmental of your own body. You deserve love and affection just as much as everyone else and you will heal yourself by loving and accepting who you are.

Neptune in the Second House

When Neptune is in the second house, you are a person who worries about material things. You have illusions and misconceptions about financial matters and security, and money can be something that confuses you. You may enjoy owning mystical and spiritual items such as crystals, angels, candles and incense. You can become enamored with material things, but they can leave you feeling lonely. You need to own spiritual or artistic items and develop a sense of spirituality around you. You may benefit by working in a spiritual career field or by helping others in some way. You may be able to make your money from helping others who suffer or by doing some type of spiritual work.

You do not particularly enjoy working with money and you prefer to not have to worry about the realities of life. You do not know how to deal with life in a realistic way. You can feel overwhelmed by material concerns and practical matters, preferring to escape into your dream world. You would prefer for other people to take care of you financially and you do not like having to worry about the future. You are artistic and creative. You benefit by experiencing a peaceful, stable and mystical atmosphere. You can experience comfort through music, study and by having time alone with your thoughts.

Neptune in the Third House

When Neptune is placed in the third house, you are a person who enjoys spiritual conversation. You need to be able to communicate with others about your interests in mysticism, spirituality, music, art, or anything that inspires your imagination. You have a very vivid imagination and are inclined towards writing. You will prefer to write about spiritual subjects that spark others' imagination. You will also want to write to help others understand spiritual topics on a basic level. You have a way of writing about complex topics and making them easy to understand. You enjoy communicating with other like-minded spiritual people. You need a level of depth in your conversations with others to prevent loneliness. You do not enjoy superficial conversation and have a deep desire for spiritual friendships. It is important that you have a spiritual outlet through expressing yourself through words, writing or artistic endeavors.

One of your siblings was probably extremely spiritual and you may have had a special relationship with them. There is also the chance that one of your siblings had a problem with drugs and alcohol. You may have witnessed the impact of addiction on their life and saw them suffer. You might have taken on a caretaker role to your siblings and felt responsible for their problems. You enjoy escaping from the world into your imagination and you can live out many of your fantasies in real life. You get bored easily with practical and realistic concerns and need time to discuss the deeper meaning of life with others. You may enjoy teaching metaphysical subjects such as meditation, yoga, astrology and energy healing to others. You can be hurt easily by communication and the words that others use. You have a sensitive nature and are sensitive to sounds. You can be easily fooled by others, and can be naïve or believe others too easily. Sometimes words can cause deep wounds for you and when people speak unkindly.

You are a daydreamer and when you are in school this can cause difficulties for you, especially when you are young. You have a hard time concentrating and you enjoy detaching from your surroundings if they feel too heavy for you. You need inspiration to learn and need to feel the subjects as spiritual, deep and meaningful. You are intuitive and have an uncanny ability of telling people exactly what they need to hear in the perfect moment they desire it. You can achieve success in school, but only if it is a subject that inspires your expansive and imaginative mind. You prefer learning about creative subjects and will completely drift away into your dream world if you are bored. Others may feel you are not listening to them, and often you aren't, unless it is something that interests you.

Neptune in the Fourth House

When Neptune is placed in the fourth house, you are a person who suffers from painful childhood memories and illusions. You were probably raised in a spiritual home where religion was a major role. What the family believed was important and also could have been hard for you to understand. There were many secrets in your home and you may have believed your parents were perfect and had one of them up on a pedestal. At some time in your life, they came crashing down off that pedestal you had created for them and you were forced to see them clearly, as human beings. You realized your parents were not perfect and made mistakes, which was a painful realization for you. You felt that you lost a sense of innocence in some way because of something that happened to you when you were a child.

You might have had a parent who had an addiction to alcohol, and one of your parents made excuses for the other parent's behavior. You were confused because as a child you were intuitive, insightful and perceptive. You saw that something was clearly wrong and that your parent would act strange. Sometimes they were abusive towards you. One of your parents hid this disease and formed the illusion in the home that everything was healthy. You knew in your heart that something was wrong, but you did not know how to express it in words. Your wound comes from childhood and this often carries into your adult life.

You may hold on to the illusion that you had the perfect home life. When you are older you will want your home to be special and you will have high standards as to what that entails. You need to be careful about sharing a home with people who are negative or unhealthy. You need peace and harmony in the home environment for your own happiness. If your home life is unstable or aggressive, you can suffer from depression. You need a sense of spirituality in your own home and may enjoy decorating your home with beautiful things that inspire you.

You will benefit from seeing your family members for who they really are. Everyone has good and bad traits. You need to learn that no one is perfect and it is a part of life. Your childhood memories might not have been all good and that is okay. You need to learn to see the truth and the reality of the childhood you were raised in, because it has a big impact on the person you are today.

Neptune in the Fifth House

When Neptune is in the fifth house, you are a person who enjoys being creative. You are artistic and will have a creative talent such as drawing, painting, acting, writing or sculpting. You will enjoy spending time around other artistic people who can bring you inspiration. You have an imaginative quality to your self-expression and other people perceive you as a mystical person. You live your life in a dream world, and fantasies about love and romance can overwhelm you.

You can suffer in areas of romance, because you always create a certain type of story in your head that may not fit with reality. You may imagine and daydream about people you have feelings for, although you never share with them how you truly feel. You can keep your feelings secret from others and this is where you can suffer. You want to bond with others and have romantic relationships, but you do not always think realistically about others. You tend to see the good in others and ignore all the negative traits. You can get involved with abusive lovers and people who have problems. Your tendency is to wear rose-colored glasses, which prevents you from seeing others accurately. You need to learn to see the good and bad in people; no one is without faults.

You will benefit by having relationships with people that are spiritual, intuitive and mystical like yourself. If you do not have relationships with others that are similar to you then you can feel lonely and depressed. You need to feel a sense of depth in your relationships. You might prefer being alone than spending time with others who are cold or unemotional. You need to express your creativity and will benefit by surrounding yourself with art and music. Music can bring peace into your life and help you connect to your imagination and creative inspiration.

Neptune in the Sixth House

When Neptune is in the sixth house, you are a person who suffers physically when you are under stress. Your physical body is sensitive to the environment. You can become sick easily if you do not take care of yourself. If your emotions are unsettled, then you will have a difficult time balancing your diet, sleep and routine. You need to have a peaceful, harmonious, imaginative work environment. You will enjoy working with people who are intuitive and compassionate. You are drawn to work with people who are sick, either physically or mentally. You may find yourself working in a hospital or clinical setting. You may enjoy taking care of others, and if you do not work in the health care field, you may work in a field that allows you to serve others in some way. If your environment is toxic and negative, you will get sick easily. Your physical body is sensitive to energy, and you need harmony in your environment. You cannot function when people are angry and unstable. You enjoy a routine that allows emotions to flourish and creative ideas to be shared.

You need to make sure that you take care of your physical health by eating healthy foods, getting enough sleep and developing a healthy routine. You suffer from allergies and might have food allergies and sensitivity to certain things in the environment. You may be allergic to things such as seafood, bees, wasps or allergens outside. Your sensitivity will always be there but you need to take extra steps to become strong and grounded. As a child you were sick a lot and probably missed a lot of school. You may suffer from depression, anxiety or other types of mental illness because of your sensitive, compassionate nature. Try not to let others hurt your feelings. You need to develop a shell around yourself to protect you from the negative energy around you. Imagine a white, yellow light surrounding you at all times when you are in an environment that drains you. You will benefit by studying cognitive therapy and how to use positive affirmations. You need to learn how to think positively. When you change your thoughts, your health will also change. This will help you protect yourself and create a greater sense of happiness and overall health.

Neptune in the Seventh House

When Neptune is in the seventh house, you are a person who suffers in relationships. You are drawn to mystical, spiritual types of partners. You need a partner who is deep, insightful and artistic. You can attract partners that are unstable emotionally and who possibly have addiction issues such as alcoholism. You can often find yourself married to someone who you have to take care of on a daily basis. You draw people who have pain and you can confuse love with pity. You can be blinded by love and put your partner up on a pedestal. You can sometimes see only the things you want to see in your relationships. This can cause you tremendous heartache at some time in your life. The pain that you have to go through is evident and has lasting effects upon you. You will become stronger from the relationships you find yourself in.

You are idealistic and overly romantic towards people who you are attracted to. You do not think practically or realistically about love and this can lead you down a path of destruction. You can be victimized at some time in your life by someone you trust, leaving a deep wound in your heart. You are also capable of unselfish love and self-denial when you are in relationships. You can sacrifice your own feelings for your partner and can put up with a lot of mistreatment that most people would never tolerate.

Your greatest test is to see others honestly, clearly and accurately. You can be fooled by others' words, actions and personalities. It takes time to truly get to know someone but all of their traits will make themselves known eventually. Be careful not to jump in too fast when you meet someone new. Give yourself the time to truly get to know others so that you do not suffer from misperceptions and illusions about the people you are developing relationships with. Be cautious about entering into any type of business contracts with others, because you can be taken advantage of. Trust your intuition and do not ignore any red flags you may see. Learn to see others clearly as human beings with both positive qualities and negative traits.

Neptune in the Eighth House

When Neptune is in the eighth house, you are a person who is extremely sensitive and emotional. You are very compassionate and feel others' pain easily. You have a strong imagination and potential to have visions of a spiritual nature. You have strange fantasies and are very interested in psychic phenomenon. You are naturally interested in the supernatural and believe in ghosts. You may have an innate fear of these supernatural forces, although you can't resist learning about them. You want to study as much as you can about the spiritual world. You want to understand the soul and what happens to your essence after you die. You may suffer emotionally because of your interests and imagination. You may feel that no one understands you, and this may lead you to withdraw from others and remain secretive. There is a chance you will have powerful dreams and it is important for you to write them down and use them as a guide in your waking life.

You have been wounded by someone you trusted, and at some time in your life you will feel that you have been victimized sexually. Sexuality is a subject that fascinates you as well as brings you a lot of pain. You may prefer to have platonic love relationships where sexuality is not involved and you can sacrifice your sexual urges easily. You may also only want to have sex with people that are spiritual and it is important for you to be careful who you share intimacy with because of your sensitive nature. The act of sex bonds two souls together, and if you share this with someone who is mentally unstable, addictive, or abusive it can cause you a lot of pain. Try to pick your sexual partners carefully and be cautious about sharing your body with others you do not know well, because you are a person who experiences sex as a spiritual, energetic interaction.

You may suffer around the issue of other people's resources. You may not receive an inheritance from someone you expected to take care of you. There can be a lot of misunderstood feelings around the resources of others. Your greatest test is to learn to see things from a spiritual perspective and trust that everything happens for a reason.

Neptune in the Ninth House

When Neptune is in the ninth house, you are a person who enjoys studying spiritual subjects. You have a great ability to daydream, fantasize and entertain beliefs and philosophies that are new age. You like to think about religion and enjoy trying to figure out why you are here. You are on a spiritual search for the meaning of life. You want to learn more about spirituality and you will benefit by taking classes throughout your life in a variety of different subject areas.

You suffer from having to break away from traditional religion. The beliefs that your family raised you in and taught you can bring you sadness. You were naturally intuitive and open-minded, and had to forge your own belief system. You had to walk your own spiritual path and find what teachings resonated with you. You can suffer from the realization that your family may not approve of your lifestyle and ideas. Try not to worry about what others think about you. You are meant to find your own path, and if that is different from those you love, then you need to learn to accept this.

You will enjoy traveling to faraway lands and experiencing different types of people. You will benefit by visiting spiritual sites in Egypt, Greece and Europe. Traveling and education will bring you happiness. You need to be careful about being influenced by false teachers. You may get sucked into a spiritual or religious cult at some time in your life. You are vulnerable to religious zealots and need to think for yourself. You are easily influenced and you can be brainwashed by someone who is charming and manipulative. Learn to think for yourself, and just because someone says they believe something the same as you do, does not mean they are without faults. Everyone has faults and you may fail to see that which can cause you undue suffering.

Neptune in the Tenth House

When Neptune is placed in the tenth house, you are a person who suffers in your career. You can be confused about your place in the world and can have difficulty figuring out what you want to do with your life. You suffer because you are unsure about which type of career would benefit you. You are an idealistic person, and have high hopes and wishes for success. You fantasize about the perfect job and career. You often find it difficult to manifest your desires into action. You are compassionate and desire to serve others so you are often drawn to ministry, medicine or the health care field. You may prefer to work with children versus adults because you feel that children are as sensitive as you. You can relate better to children, and value their innocence and openness.

You are artistic and creative and would benefit by working in career fields such as entertainment, music or the performing arts. You need to express yourself creatively in your work and you value beauty. You suffer when you are in a toxic or unstable work environment. You dislike harshness, and the normal working atmosphere can stifle you and overwhelm you emotionally. You prefer to work alone, in private, with little interruption. You do not like loud noises, angry people or too much action in the work environment. You prefer a spiritual, harmonious type of work environment. You are passive and lack the drive to reach the top in your career. You believe in fantasies and dreams that may never manifest. You have to learn to be more practical about the world and life.

Your greatest challenge is to learn how to work consistently and be practical about your career. You have to learn that living in your imagination will not help you find a job. You actually have to go out into the world and take the steps necessary to obtain employment. You may feel disillusioned if you get stuck in a job you do not like. If you dislike it and feel that it is not bringing you in touch with your spiritual, mystical, imaginative side then you can feel depressed and downtrodden. You have to find the right type of career that allows you to be the creative, compassionate person you are, and also allows you to have material success.

Neptune in the Eleventh House

When Neptune is in the eleventh house, you can suffer from friendships and in groups. You prefer to surround yourself with spiritual friends that share similar beliefs. You like to be around like-minded people that have a similar outlook on life. You can suffer from disillusionment in groups because you often see people as you want them to be, not as they truly are. You can be deceived by groups of people or organizations. You need to be cautious and try to see people in a practical, realistic way. Make friends with people who will bring you happiness. You have a tendency to attract people that have problems or that need help. You can become drained by your friends and need time to withdraw from them to recoup.

You will enjoy serving others in humanitarian missions and might be a part of a spiritual group or club. You enjoy discussing spiritual topics with your friends and like to be imaginative with them. You will enjoy telling stories and inspiring others to think creatively. You will benefit by seeing people clearly and then developing a deeper friendship with them. You dislike anything that is superficial, and you need strong, spiritual types of people to bring into your social world.

Neptune in the Twelfth House

When Neptune is placed in the twelfth house, you are a person who suffers from your own compassionate nature. You are extremely sensitive to the emotions in the environment and to other people. You lack protection from the energetic influences that surround you. You easily pick up what others think, feel and believe. You suffer greatly at times because of your sensitivity. You can feel depressed, withdrawn and sad for no reason. You are a loner and prefer to spend time by yourself. You are imaginative and enjoy thinking deeply about life.

You are born psychic and are able to understand things about people without them telling you. You are like a sponge and absorb everything in the environment. You need to learn how to protect yourself and develop stronger boundaries with others. Others can easily fool you and drain you of your positive energy. You like to believe that everyone is good and spiritual. When you realize that the world can be an evil place, you can become despondent. The realization that people can be mean, evil and abusive disturbs you. You prefer to see everyone as loving, kind and compassionate like you are.

You are interested in life after death and the hidden realms. You may repress your true emotions and keep them secret from others. You may feel that others will not understand your spiritual beliefs and nature. The older you get, the more spiritual you will become. You need to be careful not to abuse drugs or alcohol because you are highly sensitive to substances that alter the mind. You are prone to addiction and escaping from your emotional pain. You need to face the pain you feel and transform it into a spiritual understanding and bond with God. You are blessed with the ability to connect to God through meditation, prayer and journaling. Your life will be happiest when you follow a spiritual path and way of life.

Chapter Fourteen

Personal Stories from Twelfth House People

G.K., Washington

Sun in the Twelfth

"I am a Scorpio Sun in the twelfth house with a Libra stellium in the first house, but in some systems the planets are in the twelfth. The world is frightening with scary men who pretend to love you only to rip your heart out. I prefer to stay inside and don't go out much and do not date. It is really lonely and sad, but I feel safe."

T.R., Japan

Sun, Mars, Venus, Uranus, Neptune

"I have a Capricorn stellium in the twelfth house. It feels like I have a lot of anxious energy. I am a bit of a loner, feels like I have so much potential in things but don't know how to grasp it."

J.C., New York

Venus, Pluto, Mars, Uranus, Mercury

"I have Venus, Pluto, Mars and Uranus in the twelfth near the ascendant. The positive side of these placements is athleticism. Mars gives me creativity and Venus unique ideas. The negative energy I feel is from Pluto and Mars which I admit that I have a short fuse. No good deed goes unpunished."

H.T., U.S.A.

Moon in the Twelfth

"In my childhood years, my mother and I had a tumultuous hostility with each other. She was depressed among other issues. I always refereed fights with my mother and father to keep peace and keep them together. I resented her. Later in life, she developed cancer and our relationship changed drastically. I was able to care for her and we told each other how much we loved each other multiple times before she transitioned. The changes in both of us were not explained with words. I was blessed to be with her, holding her hand after I gave her the okay to go. I now know this placement was pre-planned and my south node being in Virgo (her sun) and my sun in Gemini (her north node). Lastly, my moon in the twelfth was her south node. I believe I was her mother in [a] past life and we healed our karma."

S.G., England
Moon in the Twelfth
"It has taken many years to fully accept my Cancer Moon in the twelfth house. Acceptance and humor has helped me grow. I have been told that my mother's spirit surrounds me."

M.C., U.S.A.
Venus in the Twelfth
"I had the problems that most people discuss with having Venus in the twelfth house. I found out what kind of men I attract which were always liars, cheaters, men who are taken, not available, con-artists and those who can't commit. I just set boundaries and let them know this is how I am and this is what I am looking for. I made it simple. Twelfth house people have no restrictions and our energy is wide open. That is why it's important to set limits and see situations for how they really are before getting deeply involved with someone."

M.Q., U.S.A.
Sun in the Twelfth
"Wow you just described my life. From my father situation, loneliness, psychic abilities and needing solitude for most of

my life, I have felt like a freak. I am now in my mid-30s and finally understanding my journey fully. It's been so tough and through my pain there always came power and enlightenment. It's been lonely but I know my guides are helping me from the other side."

T.T., Spain

Venus in the Twelfth

"I think it would be wise for those with this placement to remember that twelfth house Venus is a similar energy to Venus in Pisces. We have loved often from afar, but we have also been loved from afar as well. How can people not fall head over heels for you with this energy? It is the stuff of myths, legends and fairy tales. Twelfth house people want that. The only difference is that we can live an entire life like that and they can't. It's just too much for them to bear. I once heard it said that if we ever saw God's face here on earth, we would die. It would be far too beautiful. I think that twelfth house and Pisces Venus give that kind of love."

H.D.L., Oregon

Mars in the Twelfth

"I have natal Mars in my twelfth house. I have always felt more comfortable being alone, and interestingly, I am an only child. Growing up my animal companions felt like my siblings, friends and close confidants. I have always felt a strong desire to save, protect and care for animals. I started an animal rescue. I tend to want to help others so much that I neglect my own needs and desires, burying them so far down that at times I have not even been aware of what they were. I love to help others succeed through my strong intuition and endless supply of ideas, enthusiasm and energy.

Most of my close family passed away early on in my life, leaving my father alone. I have a strong sense of responsibility and love for him. Even though he is very difficult because he has suffered through much loss, pain, and abandonment, I have an intuitive understanding and patience with him. I can see his sensitive and loving nature. However, I have finally learned through much heartache that he often will not listen to my suggestions, and where I once fought for him to see my perspective, I now simply surrender and release it. I send prayers of love and healing to him knowing that he will feel the energy of that more than in a conversation or argument.

I experienced a difficult and lonely marriage, lacking in emotional connection and physical affection, and no family support. My self-esteem was decimated and I had become angry and heartbroken that I was giving so much and getting nothing in return. I felt trapped. Every time I tried to express my emotions, it fell on deaf ears, so I eventually stopped. However, I never gave up on the marriage and tried to make it work for twenty years. I sought out a therapist because I believed that he was a narcissist, and discovered that all that time my husband had Asperger's Syndrome, which was shocking news to us both.

Fortuitously, I had started to develop my psychic mediumship a few years before this, and the self-development that is inherent in such a path helped carry me forward to a place where I had enough spiritual fortitude to not only weather this shocking news, but also have the capabilities to decide if I wanted to continue with this marriage, not out of fear, but out of love. At this point in my life, I have finally realized that all the difficulties in my marriage were not because I was not good enough. I am now focusing on pursuing all the dreams and passions I had previously set aside. I have returned to writing, which I had stopped for decades, and I am building my spiritual practice, including my psychic mediumship.

Meditation has been the single most beneficial habit that I have adopted that has allowed me to surrender to the greater intelligence of the universe and embrace my inner strength, intuition and compassion. Meditation helps me release, or transmute, intense feelings of frustration or anger, feelings of pressure or inadequacies and to surrender in the knowledge that I am part of a greater picture that is more beautiful than anything I could ever control. My psychic work and work with Spirit keeps me strong and connected to my higher self, supported by the love and infinite embrace of the divine universe."

M.S., U.S.A.
North Node in the Twelfth
"As a child, I wanted to shine in everything: dance, singing, every school activity. But once someone told me any discouraging words, I stopped. I did everything behind the scenes. Not wanting to shine or be noticed. Very shy and insecure. As a child, I questioned everything from God to religion and always kept an open mind regarding the supernatural, aliens and more. I had my spiritual awakening a few years ago and found in Astrology what I really love to do. My dreams are vivid and at times prophetic. I also am an empath so I have to be careful to place boundaries between people that might not have a good vibe. With the North Node, I feel I am meant to do something in the spiritual community, which so far has been Astrology. With Jupiter in the twelfth house, I feel it is a blessing and has saved me more than once, especially with health. Right now, I am working on speaking my truth and putting myself out there more. I may not be bold, but I am trying to put myself out there."

J.A., Italy
Twelfth House Sun, Moon, Venus, Jupiter, Uranus, Mercury, Neptune
"I love having a twelfth house stellium, I really do. I can see what my life needs and use it as guidance. I think the largest twelfth house manifestation for me is the persistent presence of clairvoyance. I only began to embrace it in my early twenties, more so because it knocked me on my ass to get my attention.

I was hit from all angles with a bunch of different gifts to find my niche. Once I found my skillset, my spiritual journey really began to take the forefront.

I have the Sun, Moon, Venus, Jupiter, Uranus in Aquarius, and Mercury and Neptune in Capricorn all in the twelfth house. I will share what I believe the twelfth house lessons are for each planet from my perspective.

Sun: I'm an extroverted introvert. I love volunteer work and I love working in the medical field to help people, but I lose steam very fast and need to recover. I like being alone. I have always felt very out of place in the world, especially growing up. It felt like the world moved around me, and while I was never left behind, I couldn't quite find somewhere to grasp. Black sheep mentality. I do have poor self-esteem when my chakras are misaligned.

Moon: I admit to being pretty emotionally dead. In typical Aquarius fashion, I choose logic over emotions. I can empathize well, but that drains my social battery immensely. I have little reaction to important things, such as death, surprises, even birth (finally got pregnant with my little girl, and had a very hard time expressing how thrilled I was).

Mercury: I like to show, not tell. My marriage suffers from communication issues even though I have tried everything. I can communicate well with people I'm not close to. I feel like I can't get my point across even if I have the best listener and an unlimited word count. I suffer from terrible social anxiety. I'm talking crying in stores, refusing to fuel up my car, tearing the palm of my hands up from digging my nails in. I do my best when I'm not supervised. I second guess myself constantly even though I wasn't raised in a strict household.

Venus: I put myself last, but then whine about my independence. I do best when I'm single, but I crave relationships only to get bored 3-4 years in. I hate clingy, physical people. Loyalty and honesty will only go so far with me. I don't care if you're honest about something I won't like, my reaction will always be reasonable so long as you're not lying to me. I love quietly, in small gestures.

Jupiter: I believe that everything works out exactly as it should. I am a bit of a control freak, but more in an organizational sense. Financially, I've only been bad off after marriage (when it was two people, not just me. When it's just me, I'm a workaholic who spends minimally). I'm not a risk taker in the physical world, but I swear I have Spirit keeping a lookout for me in a special way on the other side. I am always craving some kind of freedom but I've traveled the world. I've been single, I've moved all around and I still can't fill that craving.

Uranus: I have an authoritarian issue though I greatly respect laws and regulations. I love bringing my ideas to the table, but only if I know they will be valued. I'm a little slow to change, but embrace it in any way I can. Often in the form of cutting ties and starting fresh.

Neptune: I've always been clairvoyant, even as a child. I left my childhood home early due to the things I had been experiencing. Coming back as an adult, I understand. I cross the veil between life and death, visiting spirits in their realm rather than the other way around like most mediums. I walk with them, interact with them, and if needing guidance, I help call them to Spirit if it's their time to cross. I also see energy (which tells when an entity is present and needs to cross over). I feel like my life is more on a different plane than here. I've always been intuitive, but I call it organic thought. Took years to actually trust it."

A.J., Serbia
Moon in the Twelfth
"I was always hypersensitive and very emotional, but I grew up in a cold environment where expressing emotions was not welcome or recognized. I felt distant with my mother, who

was always suppressing her emotions and had depression and anxiety. My father is very strict and not connected to his emotions. I started going to psychotherapy and it took years to get to my emotions. Maybe because my Moon in 12th squares Pluto in 8th house, which is in Scorpio. I had some kind of prenatal or birth trauma. I still go to psychotherapy and it helps me, but I noticed that transit of Saturn through my twelfth house which is happening now makes me more emotional and brings a lot of pain, but still connects me with my emotions. I feel like I am a very emotional person, but that my emotions are always inside, and it is hard for me to express them. Only in situations of loss and very difficult times I can reach them. When it happens, I usually cry and after that I can smile. But inside I always feel a lot."

J.S., U.S.A.

Sun, Moon and Mercury in the Twelfth

"I have my sun and moon (both at 19°) and Mercury (29°) in the twelfth house in Leo. I am still very much learning and have trouble differentiating what traits or experiences come from where at times. Others are more obvious to me.

I did not realize growing up, however, seen in retrospect, that I come from a line of matriarchs with narcissistic tendencies. Each generation better than the one prior, masking the toxicity occurring since it was better than what was experienced prior. Fathers are in the picture, but are enablers for at least 3 generations. (It may go deeper, but I do not know the history any further.) From my personal experience and what I observe of family prior, is that it is common for the child to not feel as if their wants, needs, desires, or concerns are important or valued. As an adult at 32 years of age this is still experienced today.

There feels like there is an inability to be close with my mother, and that it is out of my control. I have pretty much accepted what it is at this I point. I truly think that she believes we are close. We talk regularly and see each other at least twice a week, however, I have learned to be incredibly private due to years of criticism and lack of experienced empathy. As a child I was very shy, easily embarrassed, and often felt wildly misunderstood. I was the scapegoat for any error she ever made, and her 'out' for situations she found uncomfortable. She would also threaten to abandon me if I did not act how she wanted. (Example: 3 years old after my first several hour plane ride and a long trip in a car I started crying. I was told instead of checking into a hotel I would be dropped off at an orphanage.)

Growing up I was belittled for showing emotions, and became super empathetic as a result. I obtained my master's degree in mental health counseling and worked in community mental health for about five years. I worked specifically with counseling clients with psychosis. I also did countless intake assessments. (I think my Mercury comes into play here.) I was targeted to complete assessments for hospital discharge clients (great work, but incredibly emotionally taxing) because I was good at them. I would get a lot of good feedback from coworkers, therapists I would refer clients to and my supervisors. However, the good feedback from supervisors was unwanted, seeing as it just meant more work.

Currently I am a stay at home mom. I don't really know what I want next, but I am really just savoring a lot of beautiful moments right now. I am trying to be the mother I always wished I had, and the best wife I can be. (Cancer in Venus.) I am really trying to intentionally correct maladaptive generational patterns."

S.B., Ohio
Uranus & Pluto in the Twelfth
"Just a brief narrative about the generational Pluto-Uranus conjunction in Virgo which is in my twelfth house. I recently discovered that the asteroid Lucifer is directly embedded

between the two at 19 degrees, bringing an element of rebellious truth-telling to the already charged revolutionary impact of Uranus and Pluto. I also have the asteroid Psyche in Virgo in the 12th, and combined with the stellium, I believe these placements reflect and influence my career as a clinical psychologist. Prior to my study of astrology, these energies functioned as an unconscious magnet for scapegoating, both in my family of origin and my career. My experience is that this placement brings considerable insight into collective dynamics, often in the form of deep intuitions and visions that often arrive in the form of dreams. Essentially, the systems I was in experienced my presence as an unwanted spotlight, an exposure of the underlying, unspoken, or deliberately hidden pathologies of the group. After a number of crises involving me being marginalized or expelled from a number of situations (despite my conscious efforts to avoid confronting institutional power or becoming a whistle-blower), I gradually became aware of the inevitability of these dynamics and opted to work independently, completely outside of any organization, and to distance myself from family members who were unable to tolerate being 'seen'. In a very different sense, my clinical work as a trauma therapist became increasingly effective, resulting in transformative healing for my patients. (Amor and Chiron are in Pisces in the 6th, in opposition to the Virgo stellium, resulting in intense empathy and compassion as well as a positive outlet for the x-ray vision of the stellium.) I've recently embraced writing (nonfiction from the perspective of archetypal psychology) as another positive, more conscious and deliberate outlet for my twelfth house visions and critiques, resulting in several essays, an edited book coming out this Spring, and a longer manuscript that I hope to publish sometime in the next year or two. My sense is that the suffering of this placement was in some ways karmically necessary and in other ways simply a function of my own struggle to become more conscious and self-aware. I also have a tough conjunction of Moon, Neptune, and Ophelia in Scorpio in the 2nd that amplifies my compassion but also the Neptunian fog."

T.M., U.S.A.
Moon, Jupiter, Venus, Mars, Sun, Pluto in the Twelfth
"I have six planets in the twelfth house. Pluto, Sun and Mars are conjunct. I have Neptune in my second house in Libra. Saturn in my third squaring Jupiter and Venus. I have an anxious nature. I am an INFJ in the Myers-Briggs assessment, extremely introverted, but good at acting like an extrovert, even though I find it draining and always need a lot of alone time. I have a master's degree and have worked in executive leadership positions. Thankfully the Virgo ascendent has others see me as organized and efficient which has served me well professionally. I have strong communication skills and am also drawn to poetry and novel writing. Of course, the Saturn square has me always in question of my communication.

I have been involved in clairvoyant and intuitive training, meditation and mediumship. I have two children and a husband of twenty-five years who are the people I am closest to in this world. I am not very sociable but again can be talkative, outgoing, and caring. I am very empathic and highly sensitive to other people's energy. More and more I am hopeful and guided by a spiritual source which helps me to appreciate the education learned in this physical reality."

S.S., New York
Sun, Pluto, Mercury, Uranus in the Twelfth
"I have my Sun conjunct Pluto and my Mercury conjunct Uranus in Virgo in the 12th house. My father was absent for most [of] my life. He was a drug addict and illiterate but had a good heart. I am very social but I am an introvert at heart and need my alone time to regroup. I feel others' emotions like they are

my own and use my energy to help heal if I can. I was born communicating with the dead and other realms. My best friend since I was 10 months old was my dearly departed grand-uncle. He helped me through a lot of hardships and abuse from my mother and others. When I was 10 years old, I was embraced by Jesus and my Kundalini was activated. After that my abilities were out of this world. I started communicating with my guides and they taught me techniques like meditation, astral travel, telepathy, telekinesis, manifestation, Tai Chi, Reiki, and others. My grandmother was my rock and kept me on track. She was my true mother. I slept with her and when she would get sick I would be able to heal her, but the last time I wasn't allowed to get there in time. My grandmother told me that I had healing hands and the nationality of the man that I would marry and she was right. She, my aunt, and my best friend have passed on but they are my guardian angels along with my grand-uncle. My grand-uncle saved my life many times and my grandmother also saved my life in more recent years. Those of us who have this placement can take on a lot of energy fast and before we know it we are being dragged into the underworld. I've experienced ecstasy and the pits of despair. I have seen a lot and experienced a lot and what I've learned is that we truly create our own destiny. When my abilities became too overwhelming for me to handle, I made the decision to ask for them to be put on hold until Divine timing. I've always known that this was my last life and that I was here to serve humanity by completing God's will and I am so grateful to serve and walk alongside all of you on this journey!"

Sun in the Twelfth House: Suffering & the Father

The Sun glows brightly in the sky reminding us of its power. Without the Sun there can be no life. In our astrological chart, the Sun represents our main identity, personality, and outward appearance. On a deeper level, the Sun represents the father figure in our life. Our father figure represents a powerful person in our life and can have a significant impact on each of us for good or bad. Unfortunately, with the Sun in the twelfth house there is unusual suffering related to the father figure.

First we need to understand the nature of the twelfth house as one of the most spiritual houses in our astrological chart. It represents issues related to spirituality, secrets, karma, charity, confinement, institutions, suffering, cosmic consciousness, meditation, escapism and service to humanity. When our main identity is placed in this house, we often become an intuitive person. It creates the type of person that is extremely sensitive to other people's feelings and emotions. Individuals with the Sun placed here are compassionate, caring and self-sacrificing. A loss of boundaries about oneself and others can occur when planets are placed in the twelfth house. Wherever the Sun is placed in our chart is where we are forced to find our oneness with God and find out who we truly are. This very early development usually begins with a bonding with our earthly father.

There are three key situations I have observed with individuals with the Sun in the twelfth house. The first thing is that there is always a feeling of detachment from the father figure. This can occur for many reasons, but the most frequent reason is loss of the father figure through death at a young age. Individuals are unable to bond with the father figure due to their sudden death or absence. I cannot tell you how many times I have had clients say, "My father died when I was five," "My father died when I was ten," and "I never knew my father." These statements are confirmed continuously for me whenever I do a chart with someone with the Sun in the twelfth. The second manifestation that occurs is that the father figure can have a drug or alcohol problem, which makes them incapable of bonding with the child. Individuals grow up feeling detached and perceive their father as distant. The last thing that tends to occur is what I call an "absent or missing father figure". The father is physically in the individual's life, but there is no relationship and no bond. The father might work a lot, travel a lot, or simply does not communicate with his children while growing up. Therefore, in all three instances there is a feeling that one does not have a father. A deep-seated loneliness can arise for these individuals, because they always feel that they are seeking that fatherly energy.

Some females with this placement might seek it through relationships with men. This can cause a variety of problems and often more suffering. Whenever they start to make that partner the complete focus of their life, it will get stripped away by the universe. The individual is forced to turn to the higher forces for that energy. This lesson might happen several times before they realize what is happening to them. Men with this placement might feel uncomfortable with other men. These individuals might only seek out female companionship. They might isolate any potential male friends, because of an innate fear of the unknown. They do not know how to respond to other males because of the absent bond with the father figure.

These experiences are very normal for individuals with this placement. The primary reason that this occurs is to force the individual to seek one's true father which is God. There is a lot of suffering that comes from this placement but significant growth and spiritual advancement as well. Each person must come to a point where they seek a greater love that is beyond the physical. With this placement the person will find their oneness with God or the creative forces by service to others and putting this first in one's life. When the person finds that bond with the creative forces and feels unconditional love that is beyond words, they feel totally accepted and loved. This is the primary lesson that souls with this placement have chosen to endure. After they do that, then they might have the great honor of finding that bond with another physical person. This will not manifest for them until they master the basic lesson of this house.

Individuals are sometimes forced to seek God or the creative forces through experiencing suffering, heartache, depression and feelings of loneliness. These feelings occur to push individuals forward in fulfilling their true purpose. Finding oneness with God and humanity is their ultimate goal. To feel oneness with humanity is a daunting task, but these individuals are more equipped at pursuing it, handling it, and succeeding at it. The father figure circumstances in their lives no longer are a curse, but can become a blessing in disguise.

This placement of the Sun is truly a blessing for those with it, even though it might seem unfair at first. I urge individuals who have experienced the truths of this placement to know that they are not alone and that there is a spiritual reason and predictor of why this occurs. I urge them not to think of themselves as victims or believe that the universe cheated them out of a relationship with a physical father. The most important thing to remember is that the universe has a plan, and that plan is for intense oneness and love for our spiritual father. This feeling is often beyond words.

Sun in the Twelfth House Comments

"My son has Sun, Mercury, Venus and Chiron in the twelfth house. His father was an alcoholic and I decided he should not play a role in his life."
J.A., Germany

"I have never felt so deeply understood! Thank you for this article. Astrology saves my life and does wonders for processing the hidden stuff. I have a stellium of planets in the twelfth house and it's kind of hard not to feel a bit hopeless or powerlessness. I am trying to find balance between needing to be accepted and understood and wanting to leave everything behind and never

come back and connect again."
A.S., U.S.A.

"My dad left when I was three and he died from a drug overdose when I was 14 years old. I love to write poetry and you are right about feeling alone."
M.G., U.S.A.

"I have Sun and Venus in the twelfth house and everything you said is true!"
J.R., Mexico

"I have never heard a better explanation of the twelfth house Sun that is so accurate. I can agree with every point. Spirituality is so important in my daily life. We have to embrace our twelfth house energy."
A.D., United States

"I have Sun in Scorpio in twelfth house. I have been feeling so detached from everything around me. I don't have any special emotional connection with my family. I feel like I am from outer space and just a visitor here. My father was around but I had no emotional connection to him."
S.R., U.S.A.

"I have Sun in Pisces in the twelfth house and I cried silently the first time I read this article."
J.P., U.S.A.

"I have Sun and Venus in the twelfth house. The loneliness I feel is very real and even with my girlfriend and family around, I always feel alone with my thoughts."
M.C., U.S.A.

"The father figure issue is true. My father drinks a lot, usually in the living room, and I am in the next room studying, playing games and having my privacy. It's like we are emotionally detached and I also feel detached from my body, so this rings true."
S.J., Europe

"I am a Cancer Sun in the twelfth house. I always feel lonely. People always leave me. I am spiritual and serve others."
A.E., U.S.A.

"I had a dysfunctional father who had [an] addition to alcohol. I did not connect with him at all. Our relationship was toxic. He passed away a few years ago. I am now learning to set boundaries and I am in my 30s."
A.S., California

"I have Sun in the 12th house and I never had a dad. I met him later in life and found out he had addictions. I have out-of-body experiences, I have friends, but feel lonely."
V.D., Arizona

"I have a Taurus Sun in the 12th house. My dad's an alcoholic and has been my whole life. I can be really shy and detached/out of body feeling. I can relate to a lot of what you said."
T.J., Germany

"I have Sun in Libra in the 12th house. My relationship with my dad was terrible as I could never do anything right by him. Everything I did was never good enough for him and I was always criticized."
S.S., India

"I am a 12th house Sun and you described me in many ways. I also

have Mercury, Moon, Chiron and North Node all in the 12th. My parents divorced when I was seven and I have never had a close relationship with my father even when they were together. I have struggled with addiction to alcohol and drugs myself since I was 13 years old. I have feelings of being disassociated from reality and when in large crowds, I know my energy is wide open and I need to ground myself."
S.M., U.S.A.

"I have the Sun, Moon, Mercury and Uranus in the 12th house. My dad was a workaholic and I did not really know anything about him growing up. I felt like an outsider all of the time as my emotions are too intense. I am kind-hearted and spiritual as well, always trying to transform my friends and family members."
A.V., China

"My dad was and still is an alcoholic and was very strict and not there for me, I have the Sun in the 12th house."
M.K., Chicago

"I have Sun, Mars and Mercury in the 12th house. My father was absent but we reconnected in my 20s. He was not addicted to substances, but was addicted to gambling."
N.R., U.S.A.

"This is me. I have the Sun and Venus in the 12th house. I have never been close with my dad—strained relationship since I can remember. He was abusive when I was a child and at one point moved out to give us all some space. He has been a workaholic since I can remember. He has been absent ever since I can remember. It is only now that I am 31 that I can have a normal conversation with him. He has gotten better over the years."
A.B., U.S.A.

"You just described my life. From my father situation, feeling lonely, psychic abilities and needing solitude. For most of my life I have felt like a freak. I have Sun in the 12th house and I have not seen my dad in 20 years. I almost forgot his face."
M.K., U.S.A.

"My father left when I was about three years old. I have Sun in the 12th house in Aries."
R.S., India

"My father was always round but when I was 18 years old my mother told me that he was not my biological father. As a child, I did not feel a connection to my father. I always felt he wasn't there emotionally for me. I have the Sun and Mercury in the 12th house."
H.F., U.S.A.

"I have four planets in the 12th house including my Sun. I have never met my father due to him being an alcoholic and inflicting abuse on my mother. This really resonated with me."
R.L., U.S.A.

"My father was a workaholic and really into religion. I have fond memories of him during my childhood and we have a connection."
R.A., England

"My father was an alcoholic when I was a child. There was always a lack of a connection between us. As I get older our relationship gets better but we have a long way to go."
A.D., India

"Your explanation is spot on in many ways. My Sun is in the 12th house and my biological father was not present in my life

and was addicted to drugs. He has recovered from the drug addiction, and we now have a cordial relationship. I have forgiven him but there is so much space between us. I am still a bit cold towards him. Recently, I found out his father is not his actual father."
Q.B., U.S.A.

"I have the Sun in the 12th house, but my dad doesn't have an addiction as far as I know. I don't have a connection with my dad."
H.P., Japan

Venus in the Twelfth House: Secret Love Affairs & Heartache

In your astrological chart, the planet Venus represents love, affection, beauty, and harmony. The house where Venus is placed in your natal chart will reveal your emotional expressiveness and your ability to express love. Venus will show what kind of lover you are and what traits you find attractive in others. The house where Venus sits is extremely important for your intimate relationships. It enables you to express your love nature and directs how you express that love to others. When Venus is placed in the twelfth house, there are many difficulties and opportunities.

The twelfth house is known as the "House of Suffering". All issues that rule this house are kept hidden or secret. The deep secrets about your own personality as well as your emotions are locked within this house. Having Venus placed here is an indicator of suffering through love affairs and heartache at some time in your life. Almost every astrology book you read will tell you that a Venus in the twelfth individual is destined to experience clandestine or secret love affairs. How and why does this happen? This happens because the expression of love is kept secret from others. The initial emotion of love is held within and sometimes never expressed. If you have this placement you might find yourself in love with someone who is not free. This often manifests as falling in love with someone who is already married or committed to someone else. Below, I will discuss several examples of individuals that I have worked with who have experienced the intense learning of having Venus in the twelfth house. I have studied several charts with this placement and almost every time the client reveals to me that they either had an affair, were in love with someone they could not be with, or they were in love with someone and never let them know.

The first individual has the Sun and Venus in her twelfth house. She is spiritual, compassionate, and sensitive to others' feelings. Happily married for three years, her life suddenly changed. She met someone at work and instantly fell in love. The connection between her and this coworker was very strong and undeniable. The feelings were mutual between them, but they both were married with children. She described to me how devastating it was for her to feel that way about someone other than her husband. She felt intense guilt and shame for the love she had in her heart. That love was ignited and it seemed that nothing could ever shake it. This individual told me that she cried in her room each night and asked God to take away the love in her heart for the other man. The sadness in her heart was almost unbearable. She learned to live with her feelings in secret.

She believed in the sanctity of marriage and she never betrayed her husband. She never told her husband about her feelings for this other man. Eventually, she moved to another state. This example illustrates how individuals with Venus in the twelfth sometimes suffer through love and relationships. This suffering occurs because it is often inappropriate to feel and express the love you feel openly with others. The secret nature of the twelfth house forces the Venus love energy inward, deep within and into the darkest recesses of the heart. There is often an inability to express the love nature due to material, practical, psychological or moral reasons. There can also be an intense shyness and need for privacy.

There was a female client that I met several years ago, who has the Sun and Venus in the twelfth house. She had experienced tremendous heartache and suffering with her husband for seven years. She was in an emotionally abusive marriage and did not realize how unhappy and lonely she was. One day she reconnected with an old childhood friend from her past who she had loved deeply. There was a long history between them and a deep bond that was always there no matter how much time passed. They started out writing each other on e-mail, and the next thing she knew, her heart was ignited, opened up and energized for the first time in seven years. Feeling intense love for this man again, she realized that love was always there locked deep within her heart. She felt alive for the first time in ages. Excitement and energy rushed through her veins each time she spoke about him or talked to him on e-mail.

Eventually, the two of them decided to meet for lunch as friends. She did not realize what would happen to her that day and how it would change her life forever. She was walking into the fire with a bomb strapped on her back. When she saw him for the first time in seven years, she felt as though only a few hours had passed. It was as if she had known him her entire life, due to the deep, comfortable feelings that she had instantly for him. She fell in love with him all over again.

The problem was that he was happily married and did not want to change his life. She knew that he loved her deeply, but she knew it was not fair to ask him to change for her. She was in a miserable marriage and was desperately seeking love. She just did not realize she would find it with him all over again. The day she saw him changed her life forever. She decided to stop the communication with him, because it was too painful for her. Eventually she separated from her husband, even though she knew she was in love with someone she could never have. To this day she still loves this man in secret and keeps those loving feelings in her heart hidden from everyone she knows.

Many individuals with Venus in the twelfth house have shared with me that they experience secret love affairs. Sometimes the feelings are acted on and other times they are kept hidden and repressed. Not all individuals with Venus in the twelfth will cheat on their spouse, but many will have "emotional affairs" because of the energy of this placement. Even the most moral, committed and happily married individual can fall prey to this placement. I have seen it hundreds of times with clients and with friends in my life. This placement of Venus is extremely difficult, but with understanding and compassion these individuals will eventually understand the energy of this placement. Suffering arises as a result of the situations that these individuals find themselves in. It is important for anyone with this placement to truly look within and be honest about their emotions.

If you have Venus in the twelfth house and have experienced relationships like the ones described above, remember that you have free will and a choice as to how you respond to this placement. The energy might eventually manifest, but with extra knowledge you can become aware and empowered. The more I research this placement, the more I believe in destiny. You are destined to experience these types of relationships and secret love affairs for your spiritual growth. Everything you go through is meant for your learning and your soul's evolution. Try to look at this placement as a teacher of what healthy relationships symbolize for you, and be aware of the more negative energy. You have the power to make choices for your own life, and when you feel the energy is overwhelming you to act, step back, relax and try to find a way to change the future.

The positive side of Venus in the twelfth house is that it blesses you with creative and artistic abilities. You will have a very vivid imagination and intuitive abilities. You will also enjoy beautiful things and surrounding yourself around spiritual things that bring you peace. You can be extremely shy and reserved. The positive side of this placement is you are gifted and sometimes musical.

If you experience any of these situations in your life, look to your natal chart and see if Venus is in the twelfth. If it is, try to remember that this is planetary energy expressing itself. You have experiences and karma to learn and go through, plain and simple. Trust yourself and trust in the power of experience. Try not to blame yourself if you fall prey to this intense placement. It is a part of your soul's journey to learn these lessons.

Conclusion: Transformation & Healing

*Learning Boundaries, Being Realistic, Learning to Say No &
Standing up for Self*

You will heal when you realize that others will continue to take advantage of you and your giving nature unless you develop true boundaries. You might have grown up believing that having boundaries was a bad thing. You might feel selfish telling other people that you don't want to do something and focusing on yourself. You have to start to develop a different perspective. You need to develop the strength to put yourself first. You often sacrifice your own happiness, needs, wants and desires for those you care about. You can still serve others and take care of them but your life will be much better if you learn to balance self-sacrifice with self-care.

You may spend a great part of your life letting others walk all over you and treat you badly. It can be confusing for you because you are not like most people. You do everything you can to avoid hurting anyone. You would rather hurt yourself before you would hurt anyone else. You grow stronger and transform when you realize that most people can never love like you do. You will benefit in many areas of your life when you learn to develop stronger boundaries to protect yourself. It is important that you protect your own energy.

As a twelfth house person, you are very special and have a unique soul. You were born to do great things. Your spiritual gifts are something that other people might be jealous of. Other people might recognize your special gifts and they might want to possess them. Others want what you have and what you are. Sometimes they will hurt you in the process. This is hard for you to believe because you are kind and could not fathom anyone wanting to use you.

You will heal by learning to accept your feelings and balance expectations. You will avoid a lot of pain and heartache when you learn to see people clearly. You will heal when you learn to become more practical and not idealize other people. You only see the good things in others and acknowledge their positive personality traits. You try to avoid thinking or seeing anything bad about anyone. This naïve trust in others can lead to heartache and depression. You will grow stronger each time someone close to you lets you down. You will learn that people are human and make mistakes. You will also learn that your perceptions about others are often seen through the rose-colored glasses that you wear.

You may find it difficult to say no to other people. It's hard for you not to try to please others. Your kind and caring nature naturally adapts to other people and you give in easily. You will transform as a person when you learn to stand up for yourself and do what you truly want to do even if it might disappoint others. You need to realize that standing up for yourself is not selfish. It is perfectly normal to let others know how you truly feel.

You often hide your true feelings and find it difficult to express anger. You will transform and heal when you get comfortable talking about anger and the things that upset you. The more you allow yourself to express your true feelings and not keep them secret from others, the more you will heal. You need to develop skills of speaking the truth and standing up for yourself. You can heal yourself and relationship issues by being honest and direct. You will heal when you stop avoiding conflict and confrontation. The more you learn to express your true nature and share honestly with others then the more powerful you will become. Standing up for yourself is one of your greatest challenges. It may take many years before you learn this lesson fully. It is part of your journey to develop the ability to protect yourself. You will grow into a powerful spiritual healer who can help many people. You have lived through many emotional situations that taught patience. You are able to truly understand the pain that others have and helping them heal is something you are natural at. As you get older you will realize that all the lessons you learned were leading you towards your destiny. Your destiny is to embrace the truth that you are an angel in human form.

O-BOOKS

SPIRITUALITY

O is a symbol of the world, of oneness and unity; this eye represents knowledge and insight. We publish titles on general spirituality and living a spiritual life. We aim to inform and help you on your own journey in this life.
If you have enjoyed this book, why not tell other readers by posting a review on your preferred book site?

Recent bestsellers from O-Books are:

Heart of Tantric Sex
Diana Richardson
Revealing Eastern secrets of deep love and intimacy to Western couples.
Paperback: 978-1-90381-637-0 ebook: 978-1-84694-637-0

Crystal Prescriptions
The A-Z guide to over 1,200 symptoms and their healing crystals
Judy Hall
The first in the popular series of eight books, this handy little guide is packed as tight as a pill-bottle with crystal remedies for ailments.
Paperback: 978-1-90504-740-6 ebook: 978-1-84694-629-5

Take Me To Truth
Undoing the Ego
Nouk Sanchez, Tomas Vieira
The best-selling step-by-step book on shedding the Ego, using the teachings of *A Course In Miracles*.
Paperback: 978-1-84694-050-7 ebook: 978-1-84694-654-7

The 7 Myths about Love...Actually!
The Journey from your HEAD to the HEART of your SOUL
Mike George
Smashes all the myths about LOVE.
Paperback: 978-1-84694-288-4 ebook: 978-1-84694-682-0

The Holy Spirit's Interpretation of the New Testament
A Course in Understanding and Acceptance
Regina Dawn Akers
Following on from the strength of *A Course In Miracles*, NTI
teaches us how to experience the love and oneness of God.
Paperback: 978-1-84694-085-9 ebook: 978-1-78099-083-5

The Message of A Course In Miracles
A translation of the Text in plain language
Elizabeth A. Cronkhite
A translation of *A Course in Miracles* into plain, everyday
language for anyone seeking inner peace. The companion
volume, *Practicing A Course In Miracles*, offers practical lessons
and mentoring.
Paperback: 978-1-84694-319-5 ebook: 978-1-84694-642-4

Your Simple Path
Find Happiness in every step
Ian Tucker
A guide to helping us reconnect with what is really important in
our lives.
Paperback: 978-1-78279-349-6 ebook: 978-1-78279-348-9

365 Days of Wisdom
Daily Messages To Inspire You Through The Year
Dadi Janki
Daily messages which cool the mind, warm the heart and guide
you along your journey.
Paperback: 978-1-84694-863-3 ebook: 978-1-84694-864-0

Body of Wisdom
Women's Spiritual Power and How it Serves
Hilary Hart
Bringing together the dreams and experiences of women across
the world with today's most visionary spiritual teachers.
Paperback: 978-1-78099-696-7 ebook: 978-1-78099-695-0

Dying to Be Free
From Enforced Secrecy to Near Death to True Transformation
Hannah Robinson
After an unexpected accident and near-death experience, Hannah
Robinson found herself radically transforming her life, while a
remarkable new insight altered her relationship with her father, a
practising Catholic priest.
Paperback: 978-1-78535-254-6 ebook: 978-1-78535-255-3

The Ecology of the Soul
A Manual of Peace, Power and Personal Growth for Real People
in the Real World
Aidan Walker
Balance your own inner Ecology of the Soul to regain your
natural state of peace, power and wellbeing.
Paperback: 978-1-78279-850-7 ebook: 978-1-78279-849-1

Not I, Not other than I
The Life and Teachings of Russel Williams
Steve Taylor, Russel Williams
The miraculous life and inspiring teachings of one of the World's
greatest living Sages.
Paperback: 978-1-78279-729-6 ebook: 978-1-78279-728-9

On the Other Side of Love
A woman's unconventional journey towards wisdom
Muriel Maufroy
When life has lost all meaning, what do you do?
Paperback: 978-1-78535-281-2 ebook: 978-1-78535-282-9

Practicing A Course In Miracles
A translation of the Workbook in plain language, with
mentor's notes
Elizabeth A. Cronkhite
The practical second and third volumes of The Plain-Language
A Course In Miracles.
Paperback: 978-1-84694-403-1 ebook: 978-1-78099-072-9

Quantum Bliss
The Quantum Mechanics of Happiness, Abundance, and Health
George S. Mentz
Quantum Bliss is the breakthrough summary of success and
spirituality secrets that customers have been waiting for.
Paperback: 978-1-78535-203-4 ebook: 978-1-78535-204-1

The Upside Down Mountain
Mags MacKean
A must-read for anyone weary of chasing success and happiness
– one woman's inspirational journey swapping the uphill slog for
the downhill slope.
Paperback: 978-1-78535-171-6 ebook: 978-1-78535-172-3

Your Personal Tuning Fork
The Endocrine System
Deborah Bates
Discover your body's health secret, the endocrine system, and
'twang' your way to sustainable health!
Paperback: 978-1-84694-503-8 ebook: 978-1-78099-697-4

Readers of ebooks can buy or view any of these bestsellers by clicking on the live link in the title. Most titles are published in paperback and as an ebook. Paperbacks are available in traditional bookshops. Both print and ebook formats are available online.

Find more titles and sign up to our readers' newsletter at http://www.johnhuntpublishing.com/mind-body-spirit

Follow us on Facebook at https://www.facebook.com/OBooks/ and Twitter at https://twitter.com/obooks